Winning Proposals

Winning Proposals

The Essential Guide for Law Firms and Legal Services Providers

John de Forte

Buying Legal Council

www.buyinglegal.com

2017

Winning Proposals

Published by Buying Legal Council.
www.buyinglegal.com

First published in 2017.

Publisher's Note
This publication is designed to provide accurate and authoritative information in regard to the subject matter covered. It is sold with the understanding that the publisher is not engaged in rendering legal, accounting or other professional services. If you require legal advice or other expert assistance, you should seek the services of a competent professional.

ISBN: 978-0692893739

Printed in the United States of America.

Cover design by Christian Harnoth, Nuremberg (Germany)
www.christianharnoth.de

Dedicated to Dilly de Forte

Winning Proposals

"Very insightful and accurate. *Winning Proposals* is an essential guide to the role of Procurement, what Procurement looks for in firms' responses and how to navigate and win tendering events."
Marty Harlow, Director, Legal Services Procurement, GlaxoSmithKline

"*Winning Proposals* is very well done and very thorough. Every last step is covered in an ideal RFP approach - more than I could have imagined. A must read for legal marketers involved in bidding for work."
Helena M. Lawrence, Senior Marketing & Business Development Manager, Orrick and Legal Marketing Association Mid-Atlantic Region President

"A step-by-step manual for creating more value for the firms and, in turn, their clients."
Lisa Khan, Professional Services Procurement Leader

"*Winning Proposals* is a comprehensive guide to understanding how RFPs affect law firm client retention and acquisition. Understanding how to perform within the new business process, and how to differentiate the firm, is invaluable to business development, marketing and management alike."
Gina F. Rubel, Esq., President/CEO, Furia Rubel Communications, Inc.

"Legal Sourcing professionals are actively looking for law firms to take a progressive approach to the commercial aspects of their client engagements. This book will be a great resource for the more enlightened firms and their bid teams."
Sandy Duncan, Senior Sourcing Manager - Legal & Fees, Lloyds Banking Group

Table of Contents

Winning Proposals

Foreword

Winning Proposals, as the name states, is aimed at helping law firms and legal services providers write better proposals and improve their chances of winning business. The traditional relationship-driven selection of legal services providers has given way to a process-driven, professional business-to-business sourcing approach. This requires law firms and providers to rethink how they sell their services.

I was therefore delighted when John agreed to write this book. It is an essential bridge between professional buyers of legal services and professional sellers of legal services.

Although John is based in London (and the book is hence written in British English), the content is universally applicable. No matter where you practice or bid for legal services – if you want to win clients' business, you need to have studied and internalized this book. It should be in the hands of every lawyer, pitching professional, law firm marketer, and business development executive; in fact, anyone involved with selling legal services. Studying and applying *Winning Proposals* can make the difference between a win and a loss.

I would like to thank everyone who contributed comments and suggestions. In addition to a number of procurement professionals who provided a valuable perspective from the client side (see the Preface below), these included Simone Pasquini, Gina Furia Rubel, and Stefan Segadlo. I would also like to thank the Legal Marketers Extraordinaire Group for their suggestions regarding the title: Kris Berger Long, Brenda Christmas Marlowe, Darryl Cross, Trish Desilets Lilley, Peter Feldman, Patrick Fuller, Tammy Gales Mangan, Diane E. Hamlin, Amy Hrehovcik, Kevin Iredell, Jim Jarrell, Gail Porter Lamarche, Derek Maine, Jayne Navarre, Kimberly Reisman, Julie Savarino, Dorsey B. Terry Jr., and Ian Turvill.

Dr. Silvia Hodges Silverstein
New York, July 2017

Graphs & Tables

Checklists

Abbreviations

AFA	Alternative Fee Arrangement
CEO	Chief Executive Officer
CFO	Chief Financial Officer
CV	Curriculum Vitae
FTSE	Financial Times Stock Exchange
GC	General Counsel
HR	Human Resources
ISBE	Issues, Solutions, Benefits and Evidence
ITT	Invitation to Tender
KPI	Key Performance Indicator
PQQ	Pre-Qualification Questionnaire
PTW	Price-To-Win
Q&A	Questions & Answers
RFP	Request for Proposal
ROI	Return on Investment
WYSIWYG	What You See Is What You Get

Preface

For many corporate lawyers, responding to RFPs and attending new business presentations have become a normal part of their working lives. But of all the activities which come under the umbrella of business development, proposing requires the most diverse range of skills.

Apart from being able to communicate persuasively on paper and in person, these may include areas such as project and contract management, graphic design, interview technique, intelligence gathering and competitor analysis. While fee-earners increasingly have dedicated bid specialists to help them in these and related fields, everyone involved can benefit from gaining a deeper understanding of the factors which can contribute to a successful outcome.

The purpose of this book, therefore, is to provide an overview of all aspects of the proposals process and a guide to how to approach it – based on 30 years' experience of seeing what works in practice.

Proposing is a global activity. While it is of course true that cultural and regulatory factors may influence business development and acquisition, the principle of understanding client need applies in any context. The book is therefore aimed at an international audience. Familiarity with terms such as 'proposing', 'tendering' and 'bidding' may vary from country to country, but for current purposes they are used interchangeably.

At the heart of any enquiry into what constitutes effective bidding must be the buyer – and in particular, what they want and expect from their prospective suppliers. This is covered in some detail in the first chapter and is referred to throughout the book. I am therefore very grateful for the comments and observations of professionals who are closely involved in the selection of external legal advisers. This has enabled me to test and verify many of the approaches which I recommend as good practice.

Among those who have contributed include Jo Ellen Hatfield at Bunge North America, Matt Rossman at XL Catlin, Philada Privett at Philips, Marty Harlow at GlaxoSmithKline, Sandy Duncan at Lloyds Banking Group and Lisa Khan.

Finally I would like to thank Silvia Hodges Silverstein, executive director of the Buying Legal Council, for suggesting that a book on this topic, aimed specifically at legal service providers, would find a ready audience - and for her unfailing encouragement and enthusiasm during its gestation.

John de Forte
London, July 2017

1. How Clients Choose

A changing environment
The user's perspective
Procurement's perspective
Proposal models
Critical success factors

Any survey of the methods and techniques which law firms might adopt when bidding for new work should begin with an analysis of how buyers decide which firms they want to work with. What are the factors that tend to be most influential in determining their decision?

They will not always be the same. Organisations have different priorities and objectives, and these may change from proposal to proposal. There is no substitute for being sensitive to the particular circumstances that apply in each case. But practical experience, feedback from individual tenders and buyer surveys all indicate that there is a pattern to winning bids: the same factors are often mentioned when decision-makers are asked why they chose one team over another. Firms can maximise their chances of winning by recognising these patterns and responding accordingly.

A changing environment

A complicating factor for law firms is that the buying environment for their services has changed radically in recent years. Often they now need to appeal to more than one audience. As we shall see, there are some inherent tensions between what these audiences aim to achieve when they select legal advisers (although in other respects their agendas overlap). To influence these audiences, bidders need to understand how their perspectives differ.

The traditional buyers of corporate legal services have also been users of them. In smaller organisations the main buyers are often the chief executive, managing director, finance director or company secretary. In larger organisations these buyers typically include the head of the in-house legal team, C-suite executives or management at operational level. Particularly among larger organisations, the users of external legal services have been increasingly sharing responsibility for selecting legal services providers with procurement specialists. The growth in influence of professional purchasers is illustrated in a number of recent studies.

In its 2016 legal procurement survey, Buying Legal Council found that 39 per cent of procurement officers were involved in short-listing firms (although only 13 per cent were involved in making the final decision). It also suggested that the procurement function was influencing 40 per cent of these companies' external legal spend - up from 10 per cent a few years earlier.

Where procurement is not directly involved in the selection process, it is increasingly shaping the buying environment:

> "In our company, the selection decision itself rests with in-house counsel - they are accountable for the work product and matter outcome. But it's up to procurement to provide the necessary marketplace data to ensure the best possible selection decision is reached, based upon a standard of value for money." (Procurement director, pharmaceuticals)

The trend is by no means unique to the legal sector. Indeed, the buying of legal services has been one of last bastions of resistance to the growing influence of the procurement function. No doubt some in-house legal departments were suspicious of involvement from outsiders in decisions which they felt uniquely qualified to make. Being themselves specialists in contract law, many may have felt that procurement had nothing of substance to add to the buying process. And, in the words of one procurement officer, "the in-house lawyers are slow to trust that the procurement department will not jump in blindly and ruin the relationship with the law firm."

Whatever the reasons for resistance, attitudes to procurement within legal departments are changing. Even where they are not, senior management is increasingly insisting that procurement gets involved. The Buying Legal Council survey indicates that companies believe the intervention of professional purchasers is helpful in a number of respects. These include negotiating and measuring value from external providers; managing legal spend; improving the efficiency of the procurement process; and enabling more objective comparisons between firms.

Perhaps not surprisingly, a higher proportion of respondents (86 per cent) said procurement had some involvement in the buying of more routine legal services (such as debt collection and minor litigation) than in high-end, complex matters (45 per cent).

The user's perspective

However marked the growth in the influence of procurement, in-house legal departments and other service users will continue to play a fundamental role in choosing their advisers. To understand how service users choose, we need to know what is important to them.

Service users (we should assume) are capable of making rational decisions; but that does not mean there is not an emotional aspect to how they reach them. The choice of adviser is unlikely to be purely a matter of factual calculation. A good place to start is to consider the nature of the decision, and how it might differ from the purchase say of goods or more commoditised services. Three conditions in particular tend to apply when organisations go through the process of choosing legal advisers.

First, there is often a lot at stake. The selection of a firm of advisers is not a casual decision. Choosing the right team may have far reaching implications for the organisation, and perhaps for the decision-makers themselves. Indeed, sometimes the choice of adviser provides a focal point for political in-fighting. This explains why the selection process often causes apprehension among decision-makers and is one of the reasons it is important for contenders to gain the decision-makers' trust.

Second, there is often no easy way to test a firm's capabilities before awarding the contract and that increases the decision-makers' risk of making a mistake. This again underlines the importance of trust. It also explains why firms with no track record with an organisation tend to be at a disadvantage to those who have.

Third, the service will usually involve regular interaction between client and adviser over an extended period. Decision-makers will feel that they need to enjoy a degree of rapport with their advisers if matters are to progress smoothly and they are to get maximum value from the relationship. They will be able to come to some conclusions about that if they have worked with the individuals before. Otherwise, one of their main preoccupations will be judging not just how successful each firm would be in delivering the service - but also what they would actually be like to work with.

These considerations are reflected in what decision-makers say about how they reached their conclusion on which firm to choose. Five factors stand out: empathy, problem-solving, commitment, leadership & teamwork, and value for money. The quotations below are drawn mainly from feedback obtained following the completion of tenders.

Empathy

Establishing empathy with the prospective client is particularly important. Personal chemistry undoubtedly plays a part, but so do understanding and focusing on the prospective client's business and being sensitive to the personal objectives and agenda of the decision-makers.

> "The winning team demonstrated that they had understood the pressures we are under, and could apply their expertise to support us." (Managing Director, owner-managed business)

> "The firm we eventually chose had faced many of the issues we ourselves were facing, and this came out in the sensitive way they intended to tackle the assignment." (Company Secretary, architectural practice)

> "Personal chemistry was important, but they also showed they had a good understanding of the business and the threats and opportunities in the marketplace where we operate." (CFO, FTSE 100 company)

Problem-solving

Decision-makers look for evidence that their prospective advisers will be prepared "to go the extra mile" in serving them, and that they will provide solutions which are not only technically accurate but will also help to solve practical problems.

> "Early on in our initial meeting with one firm, we mentioned the fact that we had a problem with tax. Within 24 hours, they got back to us suggesting a solution. We were very impressed that they were prepared to be proactive in this way." (Finance Director, international food group)

"What we wanted was evidence of extra thought, not just what we'd told them during the briefing." (Operations Director, medium sized charity)

"The firm gave us clear recommendations that we could understand and that addressed our key concerns – that is why we appointed them." (Head of Legal, FTSE 250 company)

Commitment

Prospective clients want to feel that their business is important to the firm they choose, and that they will always be treated as a high priority. Wherever possible, firms should demonstrate enthusiasm and commitment during the tender process:

"We contacted eight firms, but only half of these came to see us. Obviously these firms started with a huge advantage." (Director, major international charity)

"I actually had to chase up one firm to get them to arrange a meeting. It was hard for them to recover after that." (CFO, FTSE 100 company)

"One team seemed to be so busy with other things that we wondered whether it would matter to them if they won the work or not. So we effectively discounted them." (Managing Director, construction company)

"They were very quickly off the mark, knew which questions they needed to ask and seemed to have everybody available when they were needed. We were impressed by their organisational skills, and felt this boded well for how they would run the job." (Group Controller, Swedish-based multinational)

Leadership & teamwork

The partner or director put forward to lead the assignment must be genuinely committed to working with the prospective client, and must demonstrate that he or she has authority and the respect of the team:

"A very senior partner turned up, but he hadn't been involved before the presentation and did not understand the detail of what we wanted. Naturally, we assumed he would do nothing if we appointed them." (CFO, FTSE 250 company)

Moreover, there should be no confusion or ambiguity about who is leading the team:

> "The team leader seemed to take a back seat in the presentation while his deputy did most of the talking. It made us wonder if the leader might step down pretty quickly after the appointment." (Group Pensions Director, FTSE 100 company)

A more common problem, however, is the leader being too dominant at the expense of junior colleagues:

> "They were very good, but we did not get much of a feel for what the associates were like - it was less of a complete team. This is what swung it in the end." (Head of Legal, financial institution)

> "The lead partner was very strong but it did not seem that he knew his colleagues very well...other members of the team did not come through." (Operations Director, medium-sized charity)

The importance of a cohesive and well co-ordinated team cannot be underestimated. Do not take people to site visits or presentations unless they are going to make an active contribution to the meeting. Everyone in the team should have a clearly defined role; team members must show they are able to work together:

> "I was fairly appalled by the way some firms responded [to the tender]. Many just did not gel as a team. And I interviewed one firm where the two partners put forward for this assignment had not even met before." (General Counsel, FTSE 100 company)

> "One presentation was hilarious – the people on the team did not seem to be aware of each other's existence." (HR Director, financial services group)

Conversely, you are likely to make a strong impression if the leader plays an active part in binding the team together:

> "The senior partner introduced his team members at the opportune time in discussions and let them speak for themselves. We got the

impression that they had put the team together carefully and that they had worked with each other before." (Legal procurement specialist, electrical manufacturing company)

Ways in in which a team can convey a strong sense of cohesion are explored in chapter 7.

Value for money

One of the main reasons for holding a tender is finding the right team for the best price. Most decision-makers actively balance the fee proposal against the value they believe they will receive. They expect the fee proposal to make commercial sense - not only for themselves but for the firm as well – and are likely to be apprehensive about attempts to "buy" the work:

> "We appointed the firm which proposed the lowest fee, but not just because it was the most economic. They'd demonstrated that they could do the work more efficiently." (Director, private investment office)

> "One firm offered a large discount without any real explanation. It worried us that they were prepared to do the work at low or no profit; we assumed that they'd try to make up for it by assigning junior people or charging us additional costs later on." (Trustee, institutional landowner)

> "When one team found out that their fee proposal was well out of line, they cut the price substantially... actually, we were interested in why their fee was higher, but by cutting it so much they completely blew their credibility." (Finance Director, large privately owned financial services group)

Procurement's perspective

As discussed above, in recent years professional procurement specialists have become an increasingly common presence in bids for legal services. Many firms did not regard this as a welcome development. They were concerned that procurement's sole function was to drive prices as low as possible. Moreover, many bidders complained that procurement officers often lacked sufficient understanding of legal services to make a proper assessment of value, and to judge prices in that context.

No doubt this complaint may sometimes be justified. But as procurement's influence is expanding and purchasing professionals are becoming more experienced in buying legal services, law firms need to work out how to gain advantage from their involvement. To gain a stronger understanding of procurement's perspective, it is worth taking a step back to consider how the function has been evolving across industry.

The nature of corporate purchasing has changed dramatically over the last 25 years. In the traditional purchasing model, all decisions were taken by senior operational management and procurement was not recognised as a discipline in its own right. This gradually gave way to a tactical model, where purchasing people were employed to sort out problems and drive down costs.

More recently the discipline has achieved something of a breakthrough, developing in some companies into a strategic function. This is reflected in the fact that many business schools now run courses on strategic purchasing. The economic downturn put the emphasis back on cost reduction and that will always be part of the procurement department's role. But there is no doubt that procurement's status and influence within organisations is continuing to rise.

Spectrum of maturity

Not surprisingly, the most strategically-orientated legal procurement departments tend to be found in large companies with substantial legal spend. Procurement departments in smaller companies, or companies which little or no direct procurement (such as service businesses) tend to be less developed. Firms bidding for work hence need to adjust their approach to the maturity of the procurement function and business sector.

> "The function varies dramatically from organisation to organisation, from low level tactical to high level strategic... bidders need to find out what they are dealing with." (Procurement consultant)

> "Bidders should take into account the maturity of procurement throughout the organisation. Many have a mature IT procurement function which may inform other functions in the business."
> (Sourcing manager, legal services, insurance industry)

According to a survey of procurement professionals in the magazine *Supply Management*, 40 per cent believed they became more powerful within their organisations following the financial crisis of 2008 and onwards. However, some involved in buying legal and other professional services, particularly if they have no ownership of budget, may still struggle for recognition within their organisations.

Tender objectives

The scope and influence of procurement departments vary from organisation to organisation and between sectors. But the general picture which emerges is that procurement departments see tendering as an opportunity to demonstrate their worth to senior management and the organisation as a whole. Often they will interpret their role will reference to the following:

Cost-cutting
Procurement specialists do not necessarily think cost cutting should be their primary role - but believe this is how their performance is most likely to be measured. The emphasis on cost cutting was given momentum by the economic downturn, but in many areas it has become a permanent theme. Many organisations now assume that the process of achieving efficiency savings is part of their programme of continuous improvement:

> "Downward pressure on prices has become a standard feature of the commercial environment, and purchasers should be setting clear expectations with their suppliers in this respect." (Director of purchasing and supply chain management, water company)

> "There's nothing wrong with the focus on price. A traditional saying in procurement is that a pound saved is £5 to the bottom line." (Procurement director, financial services)

> "Transparency and rigour in pricing has a place, even with professional services." (Procurement consultant)

> "Firms who are willing share in efficiency gains with clients demonstrate they are motivated to develop deeper relationships." (Procurement director, pharmaceuticals)

Although (as one procurement specialist put it) "some lawyers view a request for more competitive pricing as an insult to the quality of their services," firms know only too well that fee levels are being subjected to deflationary pressure. According to an Acritas Survey of 500 senior legal buyers, a third are seeking to restructure charging arrangements with law firms – and average hourly rates for London's top commercial lawyers are estimated to have fallen by a third.

Some in-house lawyers have learned to appreciate the complementary role procurement can play in negotiating fees with their firms. It may enable them to put the 'blame' for cutting fees elsewhere while focusing on the positive aspects of the relationship, in true good-cop/bad cop style.

Extracting more value
Procurement specialists say they recognise that achieving the most economically advantageous terms from professional services suppliers is not just a question of achieving the best price:

> "It's not all about day rates, but the value to the business of the final deliverable which is important. The challenge is how to effectively, fairly and transparently benchmark and analyse the commercial proposals against each other." (Professional services procurement manager, postal services)

> "It's not a question of buying any advice at the lowest price – but getting good advice at the best possible price." (Procurement director, construction)

> "Service providers need to be clearer about their value proposition. Sometimes you are left to work out for yourself what the commercial contribution of the adviser is going to be." (Procurement director, pharmaceuticals)

> "Cost cutting at the expense of quality or performance is not acceptable - it indicates more work is required to strike the optimum balance." (Sourcing manager, legal services, insurance)

Another area where procurement (and other buyers) seek value is in identifying the extent to which firms are prepared to go beyond the obligations of the contract to contribute to the organisation. According to the Buying Legal Council survey, the top value-adds favoured by procurement officers are:

1. Free hotlines/access to experts to ask quick questions

2. Free or at-cost secondments

3. Outside counsel's participation in internal calls

4. Conducting pre-matter planning sessions

5. Seminars & business level-training

Objectifying buying decisions
Procurement often sees making buying decisions more objective as one of the areas where it has most to contribute, particularly with regard to legal services. The narrative behind the claim is that service users, and perhaps in-house lawyers in particular, may get too close to their external advisers for the organisation's good. A comfortable relationship may make them less than rigorous about the quality of the outputs, or unwilling to drive a hard bargain. While acknowledging that close relationships are important, procurement is there to strike the balance:

> "Consumers of a service are not always the best buyers. They may like what they get, but will not know what else is available." (Procurement director, energy industry)

> "Objective data provided by the tendering firms and analysed by procurement complements the in-house lawyers' subjective expertise in selecting firms." (Sourcing manager, legal services, insurance)

> "Formalising the tender process ensures compliance with corporate policies and regulatory requirements." (Senior legal sourcing manager, financial services)

The tender is an opportunity to test the incumbents against objective criteria.

Partnering
Questions about partnering are common in procurement-influenced legal proposals. In many organisations, the procurement department has been in the forefront of moves to reduce the number of panel firms and thereby extract a better deal from those which remain. This usually means lower prices and extra added-value in exchange for an overall increase in the volume of fees.

Across industry generally, the emphasis on partnering often reflects an intention to improve the stability of supply:

"It's easy to become aggressive with suppliers because everyone is
under great cost pressure. You need to make sure that you do not
fatally weaken them in the process. You should be aiming to
develop your partnerships further so that they will be around in the
long term." (Supplier relationship manager, local government)

Although this may be less of a concern with law firms than with parts of a
conventional supply chain, procurement departments may still regard
stability of supply as an important area to evaluate. This is reflected in
questions, often found in legal requests for proposal, concerning: the steps
which firms take to ensure continuity of the service team; the availability of
back-up resources; resilience of its IT infrastructure; and long-term
commitment to and investment in the relevant specialisation.

The gatekeeper role
A common complaint about procurement professionals is that they often
guard access to the ultimate decision-makers, and therefore prevent bidders
from developing a sufficiently detailed understanding of the contract
requirement.

Many senior procurement professionals, however, regard this as poor
practice:

"Some procurement people have an 'only me' attitude… challenge
it. I positively encourage suppliers to see specifiers." (Director of
procurement, Department of Transport)

"Individuals have their own motivations. Some want to give
themselves authority. You have got to know the nuance of the
organisation." (Procurement director, construction)

There appear to be good reasons to challenge this behaviour when it is
encountered. According to research by Huthwaite International (Dealing
with External Procurement Agencies, 2009), bidders who had had no
previous contact with the customer stood a negligible chance of winning the
contract (0.4 per cent) if denied access to the decision-makers during the
bid process. Those who were granted access were far more successful (42
per cent) – and, interestingly, the most successful of all (56 per cent) were
those who were initially denied access but persuaded procurement to
change their minds.

On the other hand, some procurement professionals argue that restricting access to decision-makers makes for a fairer process and is in firms' best interests:

> "Our tendering process requires all communication to be brokered by procurement. All questions and responses are shared with all participating firms in a blinded fashion. Firms prefer this channel because then no one firm is advantaged by receiving select information over another." (Procurement director, pharmaceuticals)

The fact remains, however, that decision-makers are not likely to choose advisers unless they have been given the opportunity to gauge whether they will be able to establish a good working relationship with them.

Two conclusions can be drawn from this. First, where there is no track record of working with the organisation and access to the ultimate decision-makers is denied, bidders should seldom participate in the competition. (Exceptions can apply: for example, if access is denied before submission of the document but the bid team feels it has a good chance of getting though that stage and meeting the decision-makers subsequently.) Second, the very act of influencing the process is likely to increase the bidder's chance of winning. See chapter 3 for more on whether or not to bid.

Understanding what is important to procurement officers is half the battle in getting them on your side. Ways in which firms can engage constructively with the procurement function are discussed in chapter 5.

Proposal models

Service users and professional purchasers share a number of aims when putting work out to tender (see 'Critical success factors' below). But it is clear that there are also some key differences of emphasis.

Probably the most marked difference results from the fact that the service users alone will be working with the advisers on legal matters, usually on a regular basis. During the tender they will draw conclusions about which firms they are likely to work best with. The expected quality of the relationship is likely to weigh heavily in determining their ultimate choice.

Procurement departments, on the other hand, are approaching the buying decision from the opposite direction. As discussed above, part of the point of their existence is to bring a more detached perspective to the process; to help ensure choices can be justified objectively against agreed criteria. Their chief influence has been to change the tender process itself.

This agenda has been so successful that organisations which do not even have a formal procurement function are increasingly following procurement principles. By and large, senior managements appear to have accepted the argument that even relationship-driven services, such as legal advice, are bought more effectively when a degree of formality and objectivity is applied to the process.

This can be shown by contrasting the 'traditional' model of buying legal and other professional services (type 1) with the ever more prevalent, procurement-orientated version (type 2):

Models of Buying Legal Services

Type 1: 'Traditional' or informal model	Type 2: 'Procurement' or formal model
Tender process may be obscure • The onus is often on bidders to find out what they can	Tender process is transparent • Process is usually set out at the start, including selection and award criteria
More open access to decision-makers • Bidders usually given the opportunity to meet decision-makers before submitting the proposal document • Continuing dialogue in some cases • The onus is often on bidders to find out whom they can meet as part of their preparations for submitting their bid	Restricted access to decision-makers • Communication often confined to procurement or nominated administrative contact • Clarification questions required to be submitted by email; questions and answers subsequently distributed to all bidders
Proposal document often a 'hygiene factor' • Document may be used to create shortlist for the presentation • Document important in establishing credibility – but not critical in the final decision	Written submission is critical • Sections scored according to pre-agreed weightings • Outcome based on combination of scores for the financial and technical (written) proposal
Document often free-form • Decision-makers usually highlight areas they want see covered in the document (including fees) but do not specify structure	Document usually a questionnaire • See above
Fee proposal an integral part of the submission • See above	Segregated assessment of technical and financial proposals • Often (e.g. in the public sector) fee and technical proposal are submitted separately; the latter not considered until the technical part has been scored

The presentation is critical	Presentation is non-existent or marginal
• Generally the stage at which the outcome is determined	• Decision may be based exclusively on the submission (see above); if not, the presentation will have been pre-allocated a (usually modest) proportion of the technical marks
The outcome is a personal decision by users • The result of the tender usually in the hands of senior executives who will be direct users of the service	Some element of independent evaluation • Part of the evaluation carried out by individuals who will not be users of the service • Direct users may not be involved in making the decision

These points are explored in more detail in later chapters.

Describing the first model as 'traditional' is misleading in that some organisations, such as public sector bodies, have always had to follow rules designed to show their selection process is fair. However, many organisations which used to follow the more informal process described in the left hand column have now adopted many or all of the procedures itemised on the right.

The growing prevalence of the type 2 tender process does not mean that type 1 is about to disappear. But it is likely to be confined to situations where the decision-makers will not be held to account for the conclusions they reach by others, whether within their organisation or to other constituencies. Privately-owned, entrepreneurial organisations are therefore an obvious example of where the type 1 process is likely to remain common. It is also possible that an organisation might operate both models, depending on the circumstances (using type 1 for example for smaller engagements).

In any event, the decision on which model to adopt is not a binary choice; buyers have a spectrum of options available. Many organisations combine features from the left and right hand columns, depending on what suits them. Although often self-evident, bidders may need to judge where on the spectrum between type 1 and type 2 the opportunity lies; and to focus their attention and effort accordingly.

Critical success factors

While the influence of procurement thinking is evident in the tender processes and methods of assessment being adopted by many organisations, the function has a less distinctive voice in shaping the selection criteria. Senior management, the in-house legal team and the procurement function all want to extract maximum value from their supplier relationships at the best available price. And there are other respects in which all categories of buyers appear to be united in saying what is most important to them.

This is illustrated by one of the largest surveys on the purchasing of legal services. Beaton Research & Consulting's annual study draws on the responses of 3,000-4,000 buyers and users of legal services, including in-house lawyers, senior management, company owners and government departments. They are asked to rank in importance 17 attributes which influence the selection of advisers and perceptions of their performance. The top five attributes were as follows. The percentage indicates the proportion of respondents who selected the attribute as one of the significant reasons in the final purchase decision:

Factor	per cent
Understanding your business/industry	39
Leading expertise	30
Commerciality of advice	24
Responsiveness	22
Price	20

What is striking about the figures is that there appeared to be no significant difference between in-house legal, C-suite and procurement buyers (nor between the private and public sector). All groups said that understanding the business and its industry was the most important factor to them.

The importance of being able to demonstrate this understanding is a critical finding; one which is very much in line with other surveys and anecdotal evidence. For example, the Buying Legal Council survey found that the top ranking factors in selecting external advisers were:

1. Experience with similar matters

2. Industry experience

3. Service excellence

4. Familiarity with the organisation

5. Value for money

The approaches outlined in this book – and particularly with respect to developing the bid strategy – reflect the importance of demonstrating that bidders are able to apply their expertise in the context of an organisation's circumstances and objectives.

Chapter 1 at a glance:
How Clients Choose

A changing environment

Particularly in larger organisations, procurement departments' influence on the selection of legal advisers is increasing. Many companies believe the intervention of professional purchasers is helpful in negotiating and measuring value from external providers; managing legal spend; improving the efficiency of the procurement process; and enabling more objective comparisons between firms.

The user's perspective

In-house legal departments and other direct users of legal services may have a range of motivations and preferences when choosing external advisers. But tender debriefs suggest a pattern in the factors which are most influential in determining the outcome. The attributes which successful firms demonstrate in tenders include: empathy; problem solving ability; commitment to the potential client; leadership and teamwork; and value for money.

Procurement's perspective

Procurement's role is closely associated with cost-cutting, but the function sees its involvement in broader terms. Procurement officers aim to help their organisations make better buying decisions by introducing greater objectivity into the selection process.

Other priorities include extracting greater value from external providers and increasing the benefits they can bring to the organisation through partnering and closer collaboration. Procurement officers are often accused of acting as a barrier between suppliers and service users - but this is not considered to be good practice within the procurement profession.

Proposal models

One of the areas where procurement's approach has had most influence is over the conduct of the tender process. In the traditional model, bidders tend to have access to the decision-makers before making their submission; face-to-face encounters between supplier and prospective client are far more important than the document; and the choice of firm is in the hands of a small number of senior executives, who are accountable only to themselves for the decision. The model is still often used, but mainly by smaller entrepreneurial organisations.

By contrast, the increasingly prevalent procurement-driven model is characterised by more restricted access to decision-makers. The document, often in questionnaire form, is formally scored and will be critical to the outcome; the presentation tends to have a marginal influence on the decision.

Critical success factors

Not surprisingly, quality of expertise and the ability to offer a competitive price are important considerations. Evidence from both surveys and tender debriefs suggest that demonstrating an understanding of the organisation's business and sector, and the capacity to put legal input in a commercial context, are vital to all categories of buyer. Bidders need to keep this constantly in mind in approaching the tender process.

2. Managing the Bid Function

Embedding good practice
Building a knowledge bank
Measuring return on investment
Learning from experience
Reviewing the bid function
Organising training for fee earners

Embedding good practice

Firms involved in providing services to businesses or governmental organisations are likely to have been required to tender in order to win new work, and most will have allocated specific resources to this area. Depending on the size of the firm, this might range from a single business development manager working on proposals as part of a portfolio of responsibilities, to substantial departments dedicated to the task. The number of people involved in the function has increased significantly, reflecting intensifying competition and the rise in proposals activity within the sector.

The management team will want to ensure that the firm extracts maximum value from the resources it devotes to bidding; and that the firm's procedures in this area help it to achieve the best possible win rate. To this end, one of their key tasks is to ensure that all fee earners involved in proposals make the best use of the relevant competences within the firm and follow the required processes.

Common areas for improvement

One of the perennial concerns of bid managers is to ensure that teams follow internal procedures and do not squander opportunities, and that a consistent standard of output is maintained. The most common instances of poor practice vary, although it is not unusual to hear bid managers suggesting that:

- Their firms are too indiscriminate in their approach to pursuing opportunities, and should focus only on those where the firm has a strong chance of succeeding;

- There can be insufficient consultation on a range of matters, including whether or not to pursue an opportunity and who should lead and comprise the team;

- Opportunities may not always be brought to the attention of the proposals department, making it difficult for the firm to keep track of overall performance;

- Fee-earners do not react quickly enough to proposal opportunities, often leaving insufficient time for the firm to mount an effective response;

- Intelligence gathering on the prospect client, either in the form of desk research or through contacts, could be more rigorous; and

- Presentations are sometimes under prepared and under rehearsed.

In fairness, many bid managers report that their firms have become more disciplined in these areas over recent years; though they tend to agree that constant vigilance is required to ensure that trend continues.

Logging opportunities

The first requirement, then, is a mechanism which will ensure that fee-earners respond quickly to potential opportunities and that they tell other people – including the business development or proposals department – about them. Once "in the system," it will be easier to ensure that the correct procedures and practices are being followed. Proposals also need to be centrally registered to enable the firm to track its performance over time (see 'learning from experience' below).

What is the best mechanism for maximising compliance? Most firms produce guidance notes, but it can be difficult to maintain awareness of these among fee-earners or operational staff and to ensure that they are consulted at the right time. Where possible, it is helpful to synchronise the issue or re-issue of guidance notes with internal training programmes aimed at improving proposal skills. Another possibility is to prepare a tenders process chart accessible through the firm's intranet or perhaps distributed on a single laminated card. An example of a template which could be adapted to a firm's particular circumstances is set out on the next page:

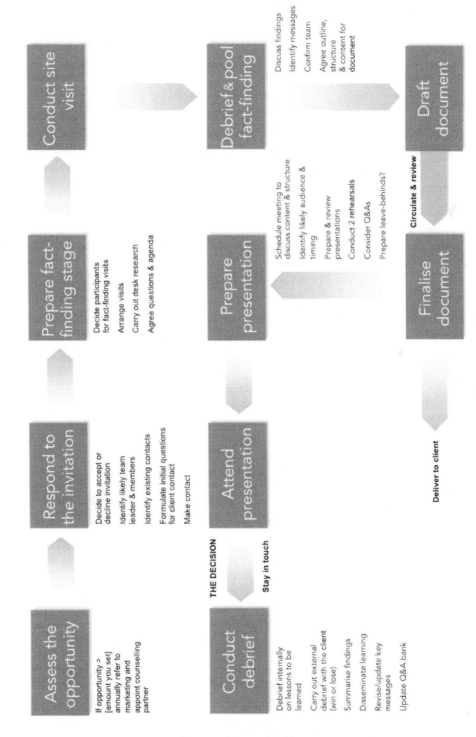

Assess the opportunity

If opportunity > [amount you set] annually refer to marketing and appoint counselling partner

Respond to the invitation

Decide to accept or decline invitation

Identify likely team leader & members

Identify existing contacts

Formulate initial questions for client contact

Make contact

Prepare fact-finding stage

Decide participants for fact-finding visits

Arrange visits

Carry out desk research

Agree questions & agenda

Conduct site visit

Debrief & pool fact-finding

Discuss findings

Identify messages

Confirm team

Agree outline, structure & content for document

Draft document

Circulate & review

Finalise document

Deliver to client

Prepare presentation

Schedule meeting to discuss content & structure

Identify likely audience & timing

Prepare & review presentations

Conduct 2 rehearsals

Consider Q&As

Prepare leave-behinds?

THE DECISION

Stay in touch

Attend presentation

Conduct debrief

Debrief internally on lessons to be learned

Carry out external debrief with the client (win or lose)

Summarise findings

Disseminate learning

Revise/update key messages

Update Q&A bank

Proposal Process Chart

The aim is to provide fee earners involved in proposals with at-a-glance directions on what to do at each stage of the process – and particularly at the beginning. By virtue of its simplicity and brevity, this may prove to have greater impact on the firm's staff than conventional guidance notes.

Counselling partner

The business development or bid department can help to ensure that proposal teams follow good practice. But particularly on larger tenders, it can also be helpful to appoint a counselling partner (referred to in the chart). This would usually be a senior partner who would not be involved in the assignment itself. His or her task would be to provide an objective view of the opportunity and guidance to the team on how it might be tackled.

The counselling partner might participate in initial discussions on whether to accept or decline the opportunity, and on which members of staff should be selected for the team. Later in the process the role might include reviewing the tender submission and rehearsing presenters.

Building a knowledge bank

Part of the bid function's role is to help develop and maintain a range of materials which proposal teams can draw on to get guidance on the process, improve the quality of the document or presentation and reduce the time they have to spend on the tender. Possibilities include:

Tender process chart/guidance notes (see above)
Proposal library and templates (see chapter 6)
Model presentation questions & answers (see chapter 7)
Model debriefing questions (see below)
Periodic summary of tender results/key messages from proposal debriefs (see below)

Measuring return on investment

Legal services providers have been paying increasing attention to the question of measuring the effectiveness of their marketing activities. The credibility of the marketing and business development function depends on making the link between expenditure and return as transparent as possible.

Tendering is an area where measurement is relatively easy, because the outcome of a proposal is usually clear-cut and leads to a quantifiable impact on fee income. Many firms therefore look at their conversion rate in order to judge how well they are performing in this area.

Useful as this is, the conversion rate alone cannot provide any insight into the relative costs and benefits of tendering, either in connection with individual proposals or with regard to the firm's efforts as a whole. There is a good case for applying a more rigorous approach to both sides of the cost–benefit equation.

Costs

One way to quantify the costs associated with preparing tenders is to record or at least estimate the number of hours spent by fee-earners on the exercise and multiply them by the relevant hourly rates. This however assumes that if not working on the tender, the fee-earners would have been engaged full time on undiscounted billable work. It also does not take into account that time is to some extent a flexible resource – within reason, staff are able to take on additional tasks without compromising chargeable projects.

A better approach therefore is to discount the hourly rate by a notional amount – an appropriate figure will vary from firm to firm, but 50 per cent may be about right. To this should be added the contribution of the firm's marketing department, based on an hourly rate reflecting those individuals' costs, plus any hard costs – such as design and print or consultants' fees.

Benefits

For the current purposes, the value of a winning tender can be treated as the estimated fee income that will accrue as a result of it over a one-year period. If the assignment is recurring, this figure can be multiplied – although it is best to do so on a reasonably conservative basis, given that the engagement may go out to tender again in the future and that it is appropriate to depreciate the value of the win over time. A three-fold increase on the estimated annual value may be about right for many recurring projects.

It would be a mistake, however, to assume in all cases that if the firm is not successful in the tender, the exercise has been of no value. Apart from possible HR benefits (enabling partners and staff to gain experience and improve skills), a good tender performance may put the firm in a stronger position to win work from the prospect client's organisation in the future. Where a firm is already on a client's panel, a favourably regarded response might increase the share of work the firm receives over the contract period – although that may not be obvious at the time of the tender result. (See the next chapter for some examples of where apparently losing proposals have led to significant benefits over time.)

All this means that wherever possible, marketing and business development directors should incorporate feedback from the prospective client on the team's performance when assessing return on investment (ROI) – regardless of whether the tender was a win or loss. Although proposal debriefs are principally qualitative exercises, they can also provide data that when aggregated can be used as part of the ROI analysis. For example, they might include the question: 'as a result of the tender, are you more or less likely to employ the firm in the future, or recommend it to others?'

Over a period of time it should thus be possible to monitor the extent to which participation in apparently unsuccessful tenders has led to new opportunities to bid for work, or even directly to instructions.

Any attempt to assess ROI in tenders activity must involve subjective assumptions about cost and value – but this is true of many areas of accounting. However, even approximate figures on the costs and benefits would help marketing and business development directors to ensure that the firm's resources are channelled into the most appropriate and realistic opportunities.

Learning from experience

Debriefing principles

Organising a debriefing with the decision-makers after a tender is well worth the effort. Apart from providing feedback on the individual proposal, it should help the firm to gain a better insight into client attitudes and gather market and perhaps competitor intelligence. The findings can be used in a number of ways, as the section above on ROI suggests.

However, often debriefing is not carried out with the rigour or consistency that it warrants. The basic principles are that wherever possible the firm should:

- Conduct a debrief for each significant tender, win or lose;

- Carry out the debrief in the form of a face-to-face interview;

- Carry out separate interviews with those involved (assuming there was more than one decision-maker); and

- Use an interviewer who is not part of the service team put forward in the tender and who is experienced in carrying out exercises of this kind.

Preparing for the interview

Draw up a list of questions reflecting the specific circumstances of the tender. Begin with open, general questions which would help bring to light any factors or circumstances about the background to the tender which the team may be unaware of. For example, ask about the reasons for going out to tender, even if they seem self-evident or were discussed with the team at the beginning of the exercise.

Typical questions include:

- What were your reasons for going out to tender?

- Which firms did you invite to participate, and why?

- Who within your organisation had a role in determining the outcome of the tender, and what was the method of appraisal (formal scoring, a qualitative approach etc.)?

- What were your reasons for structuring the proposal process in the way that you did (e.g. site visit/document/oral presentation)?

- What impressions did you gain of the firm during the site visit, and how did we compare with the other contenders? Did the site visit have any bearing on the outcome?

- How did the firm's written submission compare with those of other firms? What were the criteria for assessing the documents?

- Was any firm ahead of the others at this stage?

- To what extent did each firm's performance in the presentation either reinforce or contradict earlier impressions?

- Which factors were most important in your assessment of the presentations?

- Which factors governed the final selection?

- What could the firm have done to improve its performance?

- Are there any other areas where we could be of assistance to your organisation in the future? Would you like to receive our publications/invitations to our seminars?

The questions will need to be modified if the prospective client was a public sector organisation, as they are obliged to follow guidelines in the conduct of debriefs.

As mentioned in the section on ROI above, consider including one or two questions which might help build a quantitative picture of the firm's performance. These are closed (yes/no) questions and should only be asked near the end of the interview.

Using feedback to improve performance

The interview should be written up, logged centrally and distributed as appropriate. To make maximum use of these exercises, consider using internal communications channels to provide updates on tenders news, summarise the findings from recent debriefs, highlight areas where the firm can improve and give intelligence on market trends.

Information from debriefs can also have a valuable role in shaping business development strategy, setting the direction of internal training programmes and refining proposals policy and procedures.

Reviewing the bid function

Whether or not your firm carries out debriefs on a regular basis, from time to time you may want to take stock of your overall approach to tenders. Sometimes, a run of unexpected losses can trigger deliberations about what the firm could be doing differently. Even if it is winning a healthy share of the available opportunities, the business development team might wonder if there are any techniques or approaches it ought to be using to improve the success rate further.

Perhaps the best way to gauge the firm's competitive position on tenders is to assess all activities involved in a proposal response, drawing on evidence from a variety of sources. Specifically, firms should look at processes, outputs and performance, using the findings to develop recommendations for improvement. This should provide a systematic framework in which to carry out the enquiry.

Processes

Review the processes which are currently in place for dealing with tenders, and identify the level of compliance with them. These processes may either reflect formal policies which have been adopted by the firm, or custom and practice which over time has become entrenched as the firm's standard approach.

When assessing the effectiveness of processes, an important factor is the extent to which the firm is making the most of its collective resources and experience. Are there mechanisms in place to ensure that key decisions are taken only after appropriate consultation with colleagues?

As suggested in the previous section on 'Embedding good practice', matters such as the composition of the team, pricing and whether to pursue the opportunity in the first place often need to be considered from a firm-wide perspective and should not be left to the individual who received the RFP.

Similarly, the reviewer might need to consider whether proposal teams are making the best use of central facilities. These include marketing and business development personnel and databases providing information on the firm or on the market sectors in which its clients operate. He or she should confirm whether or not all tender opportunities are being centrally recorded - an essential requirement if the firm is to keep track of overall performance, and a means of ensuring that teams are getting appropriate support and following recommended practice.

Debriefing is another area requiring a co-ordinated approach. The reviewer may need to ascertain: how comprehensive the debriefing programme is; whether or not debriefs with decision-makers are conducted by a member of staff who is independent of the service team; and whether they are carried out on the phone or face-to-face. Which mechanisms are in place for feeding back key findings from debriefs to the firm as a whole?

The reviewer also needs to assess prevalent practice regarding pre-submission fact-finding, and the approach to drafting and producing the tender document. Who is given the responsibility for drafting and are they encouraged to follow guidelines or templates? What is the process for reviewing and signing-off the document? Similar questions can be applied to the presentation. For example, are teams expected to rehearse their presentation in front of colleagues and is coaching support available in order to help them prepare?

Where robust procedures are in place but the level of compliance with them is low, the review should set out to identify and understand the barriers to acceptance and suggest ways to overcome them.

Outputs

The review of processes should be complemented by an independent assessment of the outputs produced during recent tender exercises. This involves an analysis of a sample of written materials, including records of fact-finding meetings as well as the tender document and any materials used in the presentation.

When assessing the effectiveness of the tender submissions, the reviewer needs to consider how far the lay-out and visual presentation of the material supports the messages which the firm wishes to convey, and encourages the reader to focus on and absorb the content.

With regard to content and structure, some of the criteria to be considered include how far the documents are tailored to the prospective client (could it have been written for any client?), and if they convincingly answer the question 'Why Us?' (could it have been written by any firm?). How well do they highlight the major issues facing the client and show how we will help to tackle these issues? To what extent do they get across how the firm's involvement will lead to business benefits, and what evidence and examples are presented to support these claims?

The trend towards procurement-driven, questionnaire-based tenders may have reduced firms' room for manoeuvre in some respects, but these questions continue to be a touchstone for assessing the quality of the submission.

The firm's track record in giving oral presentations is not as susceptible to this type of scrutiny. However, it should be possible to draw plenty of inferences from the process review and anecdotal evidence, as well as by examining presentation materials and reviewing debriefs.

Performance

The third aspect of the reviewer's task is to draw conclusions about the firm's current tenders performance - and to consider how performance should be measured in the future.

This is likely to involve taking soundings from those regularly involved in tenders on what they perceive to be the firm's strengths and weaknesses, as well as comparing the findings with the messages conveyed by external debriefs. Where debriefs have not been done or are not sufficiently rigorous, it may be helpful to carry out some supplementary interviews with decision-makers recently involved in assessing a tender in order to gain a better understanding of how prospective clients rate the firm's approach and performance.

It may also be helpful to complement direct feedback of this kind with broader market analysis, to identify (or confirm) whether there are business trends or issues which could be influencing the outcome of tenders in particular sectors.

This is also the place to consider performance measurement. As discussed above in 'Measuring ROI', firms may wish to go beyond recording the conversion rate and evaluate the return on its investment in this area, by capturing both costs and benefits.

Recommendations

Putting together the conclusions from these various strands of enquiry should provide the firm with some clear indications of where it can improve its approach. The recommendations might encompass changes in procedure, or initiatives designed to raise awareness of them. One possibility in this respect is to develop or reconfigure a one-page tenders chart along the lines of the example shown earlier.

The review may conclude that proposal teams should be given additional support, perhaps in the form of updated best practice guidelines, coaching in the context of individual presentations or more general preparation through training. The recommendations should also include targets for the future, based on an assessment of current performance and an estimate of the gains which can be achieved by implementing improvements.

At each stage, an external perspective can be helpful in providing insights into how other businesses (legal and non-legal) are tackling the issues, enabling the firm to compare its approach with current market practice.

The objective of the review is to identify whether the firm is tackling tenders efficiently and effectively, given the resources at its disposal and the business environment in which it operates. But more than this, it should help to ensure that proposal teams have the tools, confidence and inspiration to fulfil their potential.

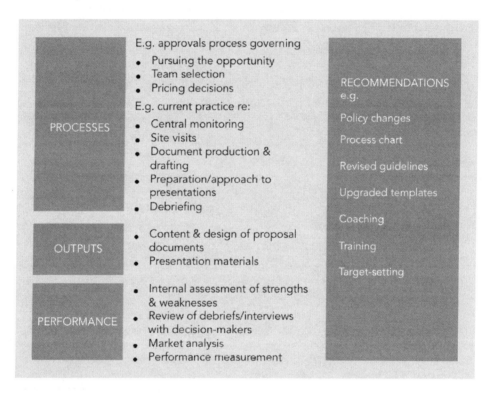

Proposal Review Framework

Organising training for fee earners

Objectives

Proposal training for fee earners may have a number of objectives. It can be used to reiterate the firm's tendering guidelines and reinforce internal good practices - particularly if some new guidelines have just been introduced, or if recent debriefings suggest a pattern to where the firm is currently underperforming. You may also wish to use it to bring fee-earners up to date on external trends and developments, such as in relation to eProcurement (see chapter 6) or public sector tendering rules. Most important of all will be the opportunity it affords fee-earners to practise and hone their tendering skills.

Scope

For this reason, the majority of the time available should be devoted to practical, participative work. It is important to draw a clear distinction between training to improve the effectiveness of face-to-face interactions with the buyer (the clear priority in the case of type 1 tenders) and training to help bidders achieve the best possible score from a tender evaluation (as applies to a greater degree to type 2). It makes no sense to try to cover both topics at once, particularly as the amount of time available for the training is likely to be restricted.

In the case of type 1 training it is usually best if the course is framed around a single case study; preferably similar to the sort of tender the firm typically gets involved in. It may be helpful if it also spans a number of practice areas – enabling as far as possible attenders from different departments to apply their technical expertise to the exercise.

While a lot of the material for the case study might be garnered from one or more actual tenders, it is usually best to disguise the identity of the companies involved and develop your own set of scenarios and issues for the group to tackle. With an actual case, there is always the possibility that someone present will have been involved; that is likely to lead to discussion about the specific circumstances of that tender – and distraction from the key points you want to get across.

The depth and detail of the case study will depend to some extent on the time available for the training programme. To make the case study and role plays reasonably realistic, the best part of a day should be regarded as the minimum.

The most critical aspect of fee earners' involvement in tenders of this kind is the time they spend face-to-face with the prospective client – either in fact-finding and review meetings or at presentations. Naturally, the case study therefore needs to focus on these parts of the process.

By contrast, training relating to type 2 tenders will focus on how to improve your scores in the submission. This is best done by asking participants to analyse a number of extracts from tender responses, to assess how they think the evaluator would have scored them; and how the text could have been revised to attract a higher score.

It can be helpful to involve an external consultant in developing and conducting the training, in order to bring a wider perspective to the exercise and to contribute insights and anecdotes garnered from working with other firms and sectors. But this form of training also provides an excellent opportunity for bid managers (and possibly others from within marketing or business development) to deepen their understanding of the dynamics which influence the outcome of tenders and how they can contribute to improving fee earners' performance.

Chapter 2 at a glance: Managing the Bid Function

Embedding good practice

Develop clear procedures governing critical proposal decisions – including whether or not to bid, who should comprise the team and how and when to involve the bid or business development function.

Help to ensure procedures are consistently applied, by mapping directions on to a flow chart for distribution to everyone in the firm who gets involved in proposals.

Building a knowledge bank

Maintain a range of materials which proposers can draw on. In addition to a library of previous proposals and templates, this might include model presentation Q&As and summaries of key messages from tender debriefs.

Measuring return on investment

In addition to monitoring outcomes in terms of win or loss, attempt to measure the costs and benefits of participation. The latter might include an assessment of whether as a result of the tender the firm has improved its chances of working with the prospective client in the future.

Learning from experience

Measuring ROI depends on having effective feedback from buyers on the firm's tender performance. A debrief with the decision-makers should be carried out wherever possible. Ideally this should be done face-to-face. Debriefing meetings can be extremely helpful whether the firm was successful or not. They should be conducted by a member of staff who was not part of the proposed service team.

Reviewing the bid function

Firms may benefit from periodically reviewing their bid procedures and approach. For best results the review should combine analysis of outputs, processes and performance. The latter may include canvassing views from regular participants within the firm and recent buyers; and in some cases carrying out desk research on market trends.

Organising training for fee earners

The main purpose of fee earner training is to hone practical skills. The content needs to reflect the type of tenders that fee earners are involved in. Presentation-orientated proposals are usually best built on a single case study in which participants have the opportunity to role play a site visit as well as the presentation.

Fee earners involved in tenders where the submission is critical should work through samples of text, assessing how these would have been scored by evaluators and how they could be revised to achieve a higher mark.

3. Responding to the Opportunity

Assessing the opportunity
The kick-off meeting
Project management

When a firm is invited to tender (or becomes aware of a contract it wishes to apply for), what are the first steps it should take? As pointed out in chapter 2, it is vital to ensure that the opportunity is promptly logged into the system. Busy fee-earners might put to one side an invitation letter or specification whose deadline is some way off, in the same way they will prioritise work for existing clients. But in the case of tenders, taking action at the earliest possible stage will often have a direct bearing on the effectiveness of the response and the outcome. In many cases a conflicts check will also be necessary to ensure that the firm is able to proceed.

Assessing the opportunity

The next step is to make a candid assessment of whether the firm should pursue the opportunity or not. You would expect the prospective team leader to be involved in this decision, but he or she should not take it alone. It is good practice for a senior partner who would not have a role on the assignment also to have a say. The business development or bid department may also be able to supply evidence from previous proposals and their outcomes that could help to inform the decision.

It is a truism that firms should not waste resources on tenders they cannot win, or which for other reasons are unsuitable. Focusing on the most appropriate opportunities is critical to achieving and maintaining a good win rate. The intense pressure for fee earners to gain extra clients can however tempt some to be less discriminating than they should be when given the chance to bid for new business.

The tendency to chase too many targets varies from firm to firm, and often from department to department. General practice firms are more susceptible than niche firms, or others where the client base falls into clearly defined categories. Some bid directors report that compliance with the firm's procedures in this area has improved. But on the whole, the trend has been in the other direction.

Following the financial crisis, for example, public sector procurement departments reported a big increase in the number of firms submitting pre-qualification questionnaires (PQQs). According to one officer in a major government agency, "we got nearly 60 or 70 applications from law firms for something which in the past would normally have attracted 20." This reflected the fact that many firms had taken a strategic decision to balance their private sector work with government contracts. But without extensive experience in the relevant field or something special to offer, these firms are bound to fail.

Qualification criteria

Bid departments are redoubling their efforts to get their firms to be rigorous about the qualifying process. But it can be difficult to formulate a clear policy and get people to stick to it. If the qualifying criteria are too vague, they will be easy to overlook; too rigid, and fee earners will say their entrepreneurial spirit is being stifled by bureaucracy.

A flexible but robust approach is to require prospective bidders to apply four tests before pressing on:

Strategic	Tactical
• Core business • Target sector • Target client	• Existing relationship • Access during tender • Price competitiveness
Logistical	**Commercial**
• Resource availability for assignment • Resource availability for tender	• Profitability • Risks • Tender costs

Proposal Qualification Matrix

The strategic category is as much to do with whether the firm genuinely wants the work, as to whether it can win it. On closer inspection, the assignment may not fit into core business or advance the firm's growth strategy.

A range of factors might influence your estimation of your chances of winning the bid. But none is likely to be as important as whether you have an existing relationship with the target organisation. As discussed in chapter 1, a reasonable prospect of having access to the decision-makers during the tender process should be an important consideration in deciding whether or not to bid. Where neither of these conditions applies, the chance of succeeding are low. Before going ahead, firms should also form a judgement on whether they are likely to be able to compete on price (see 'price-to-win' in chapter 5).

Logistical and commercial factors are usually self-evident, but nonetheless are sometimes overlooked. The firm needs to ensure that they have been properly assessed as part of the qualification process.

Fee-earners should be strongly encouraged to consider the criteria above before taking the plunge into a new tender opportunity.

Defining success

Before applying the above rules, firms need to define what they mean by success in the context of a specific opportunity. The answer is not always obvious. In an era of panels and frameworks, there may be ways to achieve your objective other than being an outright winner. The cliché that there are no prizes for coming second does not always apply.

The firm's objective, for example, might be to establish a relationship with a target organisation it has not worked with before, without necessarily having the expectation of receiving substantial instructions over the short term. Or it may wish to use the tender to establish a toehold on a framework, or receive a larger share of instructions than it currently receives from an existing client. This point is illustrated by the following cases, all drawn from real situations.

The long range hit

Situation: A medium sized firm bid for a contract with a major operator in the utilities sector. There had been no relationship between the firm and the company prior to the bid; the firm had been invited to participate on the suggestion of an intermediary.

Outcome: The decision-makers were surprised that this firm - which in truth had been invited 'to make up the numbers' - performed so well in the tender; they thought it produced the best document and presentation. After some soul searching, however, they concluded that with no previous relationship or track record of working together, appointing the firm as their principal adviser would be too radical a step. The parties agreed to stay in touch and that led to the firm being given various ad hoc instructions. Three years later, the company transferred a substantial amount of its work to the firm.

The conflicts beneficiary

Situation: A firm tendered for a government framework contract involving a large number of individual assignments. The framework was organised on the cascade principle, in which all assignments are allocated to the supplier which comes first in the evaluation, but where a second firm acts as a reserve in case the selected firm is unable to undertake particular assignments (for example because of conflicts). A third firm similarly acts as a reserve for the second firm, and so on if necessary.

Outcome: The firm in question did not expect to finish first in the evaluation, but put in a strong showing and was placed second. In practice, the winning applicant was obliged to turn down a significant number of assignments. Consequently, the firm that finished second picked up a substantial amount of work from the contract.

The deferred rescue

Situation: An insurance company dissatisfied with its current advisers decided to put the contract out to tender. Seeing this as an opportunity to show their commitment and willingness to improve, the current advisers put a massive effort into the tender.

Outcome: While the client chose another firm ('we felt it was too late to go back'), the client noticed the effort that had been put in and this started a process of rehabilitation. Having maintained informal contact, the firm in question recaptured the contract the next time it was tendered.

These are three contrasting situations where a positive outcome was achieved through a 'losing' bid. This is not to suggest that firms should be less selective in deciding which tenders to participate in; only that they might need to take into account broader criteria than purely their chances of achieving immediate success. In addition to providing an opportunity to secure a new source of revenue, tenders can sometimes be an effective business development tool for the longer term.

The kick-off meeting

Organise a meeting with the likely proposal team to discuss the bid. There are a number of issues which may need to be covered at this meeting. As with the initial decision on whether or not to accept or decline the opportunity, the debate over these questions are likely to benefit from a firm- or department-wide perspective. The participants should therefore include a senior partner who can provide a broader view, and who would not be involved in the day-to day delivery of the work if the tender is successful. This could be the 'counselling partner' described in the previous chapter.

Team selection

Who should be on the team? There should be a discussion about the most appropriate people to assign to the proposal, in terms of relevant experience and availability. This is perhaps the most critical decision that needs to be taken at the initial response stage. Being able to show later on that the individuals selected for the assignment are a perfect fit for its requirements is likely to be one of the factors which will weigh most heavily with the decision-makers. There may be other factors to take into account, such as the need to demonstrate diversity (see chapter 5). Moreover, if the team selections are less than optimal, it may be difficult to make a change at a later stage without confusing the decision-makers or undermining their confidence in the firm's approach.

A common error is to assume that the partner who receives the invitation, or even who has the best contacts with the prospective client, is the most appropriate person to lead the team. Many proposals have been lost simply through failing to challenge that assumption at the outset of the process.

Research

What can we find out about the prospective client? Ascertain whether anyone within the firm can provide informal intelligence on the organisation. If needed, agree on desk research to be carried out before the site visit (see below).

Contact

What can we find out from the organisation itself? Depending on the type of tender, there may be an opportunity to meet the decision-makers before submitting the proposal. Where this is the case, you need to discuss the pretext on which you would ask for a meeting and who should make the initial contact.

Where possible, this initial contact should be used to gain a better impression of the organisation, helping those involved to make a more informed choice about the individuals who should be assigned to the team. Discuss which questions the partner could usefully ask over the phone. (See chapter 5.)

Clarification and interpretation of the RFP

Where access to decision-makers is firmly blocked by procurement gatekeepers, you should work through the specification or questionnaire to identify any areas which are not clear or where you need further information. This will include a discussion about the tactical aspects of seeking further clarification. As questions and answers will be circulated to all contenders, it may be better not to ask questions where you are more familiar with the organisation than competitors.

Preliminary pricing assessment

As discussed above, a preliminary discussion about the level at which the quote will be competitive may inform the decision about whether to go ahead. If you decide you will, you need to make an initial assessment of the impact pricing is likely to have on the approach to the assignment – even though the fee proposal may not be finalised until later on in the process. This point is explored further in chapter 5.

Project management

The proposals department should take on as much responsibility for the administration and logistics of the proposal as possible, enabling the key members of the team to concentrate on how to convince the decision-makers that yours is the right firm for the assignment.

Project management responsibilities may include:

- Setting up internal meetings (e.g. pre- and post- site visits, presentation rehearsals etc.) and co-ordinating the exchange of material between team members;

- Briefing the library/knowledge managers/analysts to provide a pack of information on the prospective client;

- Organising the review process and briefing those involved in reviewing the document and critiquing the presentation;

- Setting drafting and production deadlines for the document, and making sure that team members are aware of them.

Draw up a list of actions and agree who will be responsible for each. Using a checklist of this kind is of particular importance in high value tenders, involving the coordination of multiple contributors and inputs.

CHECKLIST: Project Management

Action No.	Action	Responsibility	Deadline
1	Inform proposals department of invitation to tender	Recipient of invitation	Immediately
2	Circulate internally details of invitation to tender to identify links/contacts/relevant	Bid manager	
3	Identify team leader and decide whether or not to bid	Managing/counselling partner, bid manager	
4	Contact the organisation to establish and confirm the proposal process	Team leader	
5	Agree on internal process	Team leader and bid manager	
6	Identify proposal team	Team leader and bid manager	
7	Carry out background research	Bid manager/analyst	
8	Distribute research data to proposal team	Bid manager	
9	Hold pre-scoping planning meeting	Proposal team and bid manager	
10	Hold scoping visit	Proposal team	
11	Hold scoping debrief/document briefing meeting	Proposal team and bid manager	
12	Draft the proposal document and covering letter	Bid manager/team/designated writers	
13	Give final approval of the document and covering letter	Team leader and bid manager	
14	Ensure timely delivery of the proposal	Bid manager	
15	Presentation preparation and rehearsals	Proposal team and bid manager	

16	Presentation	Proposal team	
17	External debrief following decision	Bid manager/consultant	
18	Proposal review and internal debrief	Team leader and bid manager	

Chapter 3 at a glance:
Responding to the Opportunity

Assessing the opportunity

Before embracing an opportunity, the firm needs to decide if: this is work it really wants; it has the resources available to make an effective bid and to carry out the work; it has a reasonable chance of success; and it makes sense commercially.

The kick-off meeting

Topics to be discussed at the initial meeting will include: team selection; methods of finding out more about the prospective client; and the approach to making initial contact and arranging a meeting with decision-makers, where this is a possibility. Participants should also touch on pricing issues, making a preliminary assessment of what they think is likely to be a competitive rate for the instruction.

In the case of more formal type 2 tenders the meeting should be used to work through the questions – identifying those which require clarification, or agreeing in outline how they should addressed.

To bring a degree of objectivity to decision-making, it is helpful to include a senior member of staff who will not be part of the prospective team for the assignment.

Project management

Particularly on larger tenders, a member of the bid department (or other nominee who is not a member of the proposed service team) should be designated as project manager. His or her role will include creating interior deadlines in the lead up to the ultimate delivery of the outputs. This will cover areas such as: conflicts checks; desk research; document drafting and review; site visit preparation; design input, where required; and presentation rehearsals.

4. Fact-Finding and Intelligence

Understanding the context of the proposal
Desk research
Fact-finding meetings

Understanding the context of the proposal

Decision-makers view bidders and their proposals through the prism of their own circumstances, priorities and experience. An understanding of the context of the proposal is therefore often essential.

The context feeds directly into the factors which are so often influential in determining the outcome (see chapter 1). For example, it is indispensable in showing empathy and building rapport. Demonstrating problem-solving ability is predicated on knowing which issues the prospective client really cares and worries about. Taking the trouble to find out what matters most to the organisation will often be interpreted as a sign of commitment.

Taking a long-term view across industry, there is also strong evidence that 'understanding the client's business' has grown in importance as a factor influencing the selection of suppliers in general.

For example, in 2008 the US-based consulting firm rogenSi asked more than 3,000 executives involved in bidding for multi-million dollar accounts about the factors they thought were most significant in winning business. In one question, recipients were asked to indicate the relative importance of four factors: the best technical solution; chemistry between the bidding team and the client; understanding of the client's business; and politics. This was the same question which the founder of the company had asked in 1975. When the responses were aggregated, the result was as follows:

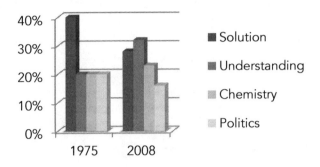

Understanding Context

According to both the 1975 and the 2008 survey, all four factors have a significant bearing on the outcome. But over 30 years, 'understanding the customer' has replaced 'the best technical solution' as the most important. This may reflect the fact that in a more complex business world, finding an approach which matches the organisation's culture and specific circumstances has become critical in achieving the best result. This is as likely to apply to the provision of legal services as to anything else.

In both the public and private sectors 'understanding the requirement' is often one of the formal criteria by which the bid is evaluated - usually with a significant weighting.

To develop a thorough understanding of the context of the proposal, having an existing business relationship or personal contacts with the organisation can of course be very helpful. Firms in such a position have a big advantage over those where no such relationship exists. But desk research can play a key role in deepening your knowledge of the organisation.

Desk research

Desk research is important, particularly if your personal contacts with the organisation are limited. It often enables bidders to ask more probing questions and therefore elicit better information from the organisation itself.

One approach is to analyse the target organisation in four stages, as indicated in the diagram below:

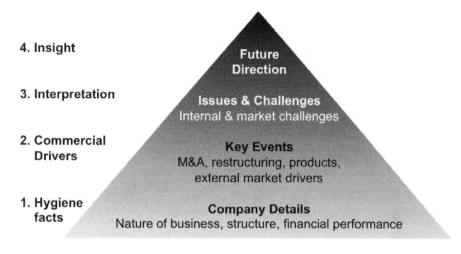

4. Insight

Future Direction

3. Interpretation

Issues & Challenges
Internal & market challenges

2. Commercial Drivers

Key Events
M&A, restructuring, products, external market drivers

1. Hygiene facts

Company Details
Nature of business, structure, financial performance

Levels of Intelligence Pyramid

Source: Brook Intelligence Centre, London

Hygiene facts

With (free) access to rich information sources, including company websites, annual reports and business sites, it should be easy to create the foundations of the information-gathering phase. That said, many firms pull off a general report and stop there. A good analyst will investigate further. He or she will cut through the marketing paraphernalia.

Up-to-date and comparative financials provide a good picture. As well as current and historic revenue and profit comparatives, delving deeper into the numbers will tell you which operations and markets are significant to the company and any secrets the company is hiding in the notes to the accounts. The analyst should also be able to give you some reasons to explain good or bad performance.

Commercial drivers

An analyst needs to piece together clues to find out what is driving the company's behaviour and to understand its intentions. Analysing M&A, restructurings, major people changes, product launches and markets entered or exited all provide valuable information about a company's strategy.
A comprehensive overview will draw on information from a range of sources, many of which are subscription based. Examples include Datamonitor,

Business Monitor International, LexisAdvance and IBIS World. Other potentially helpful reference points include broker reports, press coverage, business sites (such as Reuters and Bloomberg), financial databases and investor pages.

Look beyond the company itself to understand how the market in which it operates affects the organisation. The aim is not to make you a sector expert overnight, but to enable you to ask intelligent questions. Asking the prospect how it intends to cope in a market where margins are expected to contract by 10 per cent in the next five years, or where new entrants will increase competition, shows interest in the business and commercial aptitude.

While investigating the organisation's market profile, it will also be helpful to look at its legal track record – in particular, cases it and its competitors have been involved in, and which law firms were instructed. Reports and analytical tools in this area are available from suppliers such as Lex Machina.

It takes patience and inquisitiveness to sift through tomes of information to identify critical themes. This is not simply a process of finding and listing relevant events; it requires an understanding of how these events link together, presented as a coherent narrative.

Interpretation

Usually by this point you will find yourself knee-deep in information. It is important to take a step back and take a broad view of what you have found. The real value is providing a single report that brings together all the key points in one place. A SWOT analysis (strengths, weaknesses, opportunities, and threats) is still one of the best ways to present a succinct interpretation of your findings.

Insight

Drawing on your conclusions at the interpretation phase, you should now be able to put forward a hypothesis about the company's strategic direction and what its priorities are. It should enable you to see below the surface of the rather bland statements that companies tend to make about their objectives in their annual reports. The challenge is to find evidence to show how well or poorly the company is doing in meeting these objectives.

You will then be in a position to start creating some linkages between the issues facing the company and potential areas of opportunity for the firm. At the very least, it will highlight areas which the proposal team should explore in order to deepen further its understanding of the organisation.

Some illustrations are set out below:

A major bank

In the process of implementing a £2.5bn cost reduction programme. This includes reducing staff numbers by around 16,000. Two years previously it had announced that it would cut an additional 3,700 jobs from its branch network (or 14 per cent of its total branch staff). It is also reviewing its global property portfolio, estimated to be worth £4bn. A year ago the bank reported it was considering a £350m sale and leaseback for one its office complexes. Further, it plans to invest in excess of £6bn over the next five years improving IT and systems.

Potential issues: employment, corporate restructuring, real estate, IT procurement

A global design and engineering consultancy

Involved in several high-profile projects in the Middle East, accounting for 12 per cent of revenues and around 18 per cent of its workforce. The consultancy is exposed to late payments and credit risks from a number of Dubai-based clients and recently said it had set aside €10m for bad debts. Its chairman recently stated: "confidence has yet to fully return in the Middle East." Staff numbers in the Middle East were reduced by 500 as a result of the economic difficulties in the region (rationalisation costing €3m).

Potential issues: systems & controls in Middle East operations, local regulation

A media group

In the first nine months of the year, the media group completed 11 acquisitions which were largely debt financed. In the third quarter, the group's net debt was $3.5bn, up $1.2bn compared to the same time last year, taking net financing costs to $90m compared with $64m in the previous year. The group's cost of financing has increased particularly in relation to euro and sterling denominated debt - both have appreciated against dollar. The group's senior unsecured debt rating was downgraded by ratings agency Moody's to one level above junk (Baa3). For the next financial year the group has said it will limit acquisitions to $100m.

Potential issues: re-financing, treasury operations, M&A

Good intelligence can make a substantial difference to how your prospective client perceives you throughout the pitch process, from initial discussions to the final presentation. Many businesses still underestimate the time and skill it takes to sift through superfluous information. An abundance of facts exists on most companies; the analyst has to focus on ensuring information is up-to-date and relevant and provides real insight.

Facts need to be linked together and developed around the narrative of the issues the company is facing and where it is going. This will lay the foundations for creating a persuasive case which links the organisation's needs with your ability to deliver solutions (see chapter 5).

In many firms, intelligence is still not effectively disseminated and used. When the CEO of a major listed company recently asked a group of its lawyers if they knew its latest financial results, only a few hands were raised among an audience of over 50 – much to the CEO's disappointment.

In another case, a global financial company was approached by a law firm which suggested the company needed to take steps to protect its position in a jurisdiction it had just entered. This put the incumbent advisers on the back foot, as they were not even aware that their client had moved into the new country. Both examples illustrate that clients expect their advisers (and prospective advisers) to keep abreast of their affairs.

However – at least in the private sector – most important of all are the opportunities you may be given to meet the organisation and discuss the assignment before submitting the bid. This is a critical part of the process and one which warrants careful preparation.

Fact-finding meetings

The character and format of pre-submission meetings, site visits or scoping sessions vary considerably from sector to sector and even from tender to tender, so it is difficult to generalise about how they should be approached. But It Is worth keeping in mind some general principles.

Buyers of legal services often make no provision for a pre-submission meeting; they may feel that their invitation to tender provides enough explanation of what they are trying to achieve and the scope of the services that are required. It is, however, very unlikely that you will be able to glean enough about the context of the bid from the RFP or ITT alone. Therefore, and as explained in the previous chapter, one of the lead partner's most urgent tasks having seen the tender documentation is to identify areas which require clarification or where further information would be helpful in order to develop an effective response.

The request for further information or clarification can often be used to build dialogue with the organisation – and as a pretext for a meeting or at least a phone call with the decision-makers. Of course, opportunities to do that are more restricted with type 2 tenders (particularly in the public sector), where the only sort of pre-submission meeting you are likely to get is one organised by the procurement department for the benefit of all firms that are tendering.

As discussed in chapter 1, some procurement departments believe that part of their duty is to act as gatekeepers between decision-makers and bidders. However, there is a growing realisation among public bodies and corporates that bidders will produce better proposals if they are given proper access to the organisation before they have to produce their submission. Firms should therefore at least try to establish a dialogue.

In any case, take advantage of any pre-submission meeting that is offered. They are likely to provide the best insights into how to approach the tender – better than the RFP document itself or independent research. Failure to take up the opportunity may also be construed as indicating a lack of interest or enthusiasm in the assignment.

Arrange meetings as early on as possible, as this may send a message about the firm's appetite for the assignment and its ability to respond quickly. Early contact will also give the team more time to develop its ideas.

Ask for a scoping meeting even where the prospective client does not appear to have made provision for one, unless it has expressly ruled this out. There have been many instances where teams have made a strong impression and gained a significant advantage from attending such a meeting, even though the client had not originally foreseen any requirement for it. As suggested above, when making initial contact the team leader should be armed with good questions and be ready to justify why a meeting would be of value.

CHECKLIST: Fact-finding Meetings

Before the meeting:

Review what you already know about the organisation

Draw on desk research or other available sources of information to develop initial thoughts about the prospect client, with a view to testing these ideas at the visit.

Identify specific questions

These are likely to relate to the context of the tender, issues which you believe are of importance to the prospective client, the scope of the project and areas in the RFP where you would like clarification.

Develop an agenda (see below)

This may be purely for your own purposes, or you may decide to use it openly in the meeting. Sending a proposed agenda in advance, welcoming suggestions from you client contact, can be a helpful way of initiating dialogue.

Decide team member roles

Get the team together beforehand to decide the main issues to be covered and who is going to handle which areas at the meeting.

Anticipate questions
Consider the questions you may be asked at the meeting, and how the team should answer them.

At the meeting:

Establish clearly team members' identities

Your team leader should use the meeting to get across team members' credentials and why they are relevant to the assignment. He or she should orchestrate the discussion, ensuring that every team member contributes.

Discuss the issues facing the prospective client

The principal objective of the site visit is to identify issues of concern to the client. Discussing the client's business objectives and challenges will help you to establish rapport with the decision-makers and put the tender into a broader context.

Ask questions which build on your research

A question such as: 'Have you been affected by the downturn in the technology sector?' is more likely to encourage dialogue than if you merely ask: 'What issues are you facing?' Moreover, people are more willing to divulge sensitive or private information if they feel you already have half the answer. Show that you have done your homework, and avoid asking for information that you could have acquired from other sources.

Identify decision-makers

Try to identify who will be involved in taking the decision, and the individual concerns and priorities of each decision-maker. As discussed in chapter 1, the CEO is likely to have different concerns from the head of legal or company secretary; and their concerns will be different from those of the procurement department. You need to gather information which will help you develop appealing messages for each relevant constituency.

Be ready to change tack

Although there will be a number of items you wish to cover at the meeting, be flexible if you hit on a topic which is clearly of great interest to the prospective client. Explore it in as much depth as you can.

Show interest in the business

Apart from demonstrating knowledge of the organisation's industry, show curiosity about how the business operates. This is where effective desk research can pay dividends in showing you have done your homework. Where appropriate, ask to be shown round the premises.

After the meeting:

Hold a debrief

Shortly afterwards, get the members of the team together to discuss the findings from the visit. Also use this meeting to brainstorm ideas and develop the main themes for the proposal document.

Get feedback from the prospective client on our proposed team

You should consider getting a senior partner or director who is not on the proposed service team to phone the prospective client after the site visit. This presents a valuable opportunity to check that he or she is happy with the people you are putting forward – before it is too late.

Agendas

It will not always be appropriate to send an agenda in advance of the site visit, but doing so has advantages - it shows that you have begun to think about the client's needs and intend to address them in a structured way. Points to bear in mind:

- Include details of who is attending the meeting from your firm and from the client organisation (if known).

- Do not allow the agenda to be over-prescriptive or cluttered with too many points, but include sufficient detail to show that you have already identified some of the issues which are likely to be of concern to the organisation.

- Group the individual items under sub-headings, to show that you intend to tackle the meeting in a logical way.

- Structure the agenda so that you are able to begin with a general discussion about the client's business and objectives.

- Aim to cover points concerning service delivery and the proposal process towards the end of the meeting – the interviewee is more likely to be open about relatively sensitive issues (for example, limitations of the current service; fee issues; which other firms have been invited, and why) once a rapport has been established.

A broad illustration of the points you may want to cover in a site visit agenda is shown below.

CHECKLIST: Site Visit Agenda

Meeting to be held at [time] on [date] at [venue]

X company: [name], [title]; [name] [title],

Firm: [name], [role on the assignment]; [name], [role on the assignment]

Context

- X Company's business objectives and strategy
- Objectives of the project/service

Key issues

- [   ]
- [   ]
- [   ]
- [   ]

Service delivery

- Strengths and weaknesses of current service
- Requirements for the future

Tender process

- Evaluation criteria
- Decision-makers
- Access
- Timetable

By inviting the recipients to comment on the draft agenda and to add any items which they think should be included, you will begin to create a dialogue with the decision-makers and learn more about the issues which are important to them.

Chapter 4 at a glance:
Fact-Finding and Intelligence

Understanding the context of the proposal

Proposal teams need to find out as much as they can about the circumstances and objectives of the organisation, and the commercial context in which the tender is being conducted. The ability to demonstrate such an understanding is often a key factor in determining the outcome.

Desk research

Via websites and other sources a good deal of information is available on most organisations. The challenge for researchers is to unearth material which will provide a genuine insight into the organisation's key concerns and strategic direction.

Desk research is important not only in enabling proposals teams to build up a more detailed picture of the organisation; it should also help them to ask more probing questions about the tender.

Fact-finding meetings

Team leaders should wherever possible meet decision-makers to discuss the tender in advance of submitting the document. While the principal purpose of such a meeting is to find out more about the decision-makers' objectives, it is also an opportunity to establish rapport and begin building the relationship.

The submission of a draft agenda in advance can be helpful in surfacing the decision-makers' priorities and concerns. The purpose of agendas is to focus the discussion on areas that will enable the team to deliver a better tender document or presentation. They should not however be so prescriptive as to pre-empt issues which decision-makers may wish to raise.

5. Developing the Bid Strategy

Win themes
The anatomy of persuasion
Engaging with procurement
Notes for re-bidders
Pricing

Win themes

Bid teams are more likely to be successful if they can articulate clearly why their firm is the right one to be selected, and are able to construct a narrative which supports this claim.

Having gathered evidence from independent research and (where possible) from direct contact with the target organisation, a good place to start is to review what you have learned about its requirements. Questions to consider include:

CHECKLIST: Understanding the Client

What is the prospective client's overall business objectives and strategy?

How will the service/assignment contribute to the fulfilment of the objectives and strategy?

Why have they put the service out to tender (if applicable)?

What are they looking for from the relationship?

What are the prospective client's overall expectations of the service or assignment, and what it can deliver for the organisation?

Against which criteria will the organisation measure the success of the service or assignment – and of the service provider?

What are the issues that will affect the performance of the contract and the value and benefits gained by the organisation?

These questions will be easier to answer if the team has an existing relationship with the prospective client or has been able to establish a dialogue with the decision-makers. It is one of the reasons that incumbents often start the tender with a significant advantage. But even without a detailed knowledge of the organisation, answer these questions as best as you can. Your conclusions will create the foundations on which to build the win themes.

It is likely that you already have some idea what the win themes could be, having applied the criteria outlined in chapter 3 on whether or not to pursue the opportunity. Armed with as much information as you have been able to obtain about the organisation, it is time to begin clarifying and refining these themes. Although this may continue throughout the proposal process, framing them now will help to steer your approach to the submission and presentation.

Taking into account the answers to the questions above, a win theme should encapsulate both a need which you have identified as being important to the organisation, and evidence that you are able to satisfy that need. You should be able to express it in a sentence or short paragraph. The following statements could qualify as win themes – assuming that the authors have interpreted the organisation's requirements correctly:

> 'We can ensure patent protections are in place well within your deadline, drawing on pharma IP specialists in every country where you operate and co-ordinated through a single point of contact in New York.'

> 'Your aim is to minimise the costs of employee disputes by improving divisional managers' awareness of compliance obligations. Our training programmes have led to a 20 per cent reduction in disputes in other construction companies and we will tailor these to reflect the risks you have identified.'

> 'Over the last three years we have predicted non-contentious external legal costs within a five per cent margin and we will draw on this experience to ensure continuing predictability of legal spend.'

A win theme could be fashioned around almost any topic, as long as it is likely to be of sufficient importance to the prospective client to influence the outcome. Of course, your firm's capabilities and ability to deliver must be tied to the organisation's need. The more specific you can be - both in terms of what the organisation wants, and what you say your team will achieve – the more impact the statement is likely to have.

Create no more than three or four win themes: do not dilute key points by having too many of them. If you believe you have more than this, choose the ones which you believe to be the most important. It is also helpful to think about how the win themes could be consolidated into a single statement, which would convey effectively why you are the right firm to be selected.

Competitive factors

In order to win, you have to establish the link between client need and your ability to deliver. But you also have to convince the decision-makers that you can achieve better outcomes than the other contenders. In formulating your win themes you need to take into account your competitive strengths and weaknesses. It can be helpful to commit them to paper, for example by using a matrix:

	Strengths	Weaknesses
Us		
Competitor 1		
Competitor 2		
Competitor 3		

It may even be possible to map out a more detailed analysis of competitive strengths and weaknesses.

CHECKLIST: Strengths & Weaknesses

	Our firm	Competitors (where known)
Response to issues, e.g. • Reducing legal costs • Better risk management • Enhancing efficiency through knowledge sharing • Delivering within tighter timeframes • Enhancing the commerciality of advice	Our firm	Competitors (where known)
Team credentials, e.g. • Overall experience • Range and balance of resources • Comparable project experience • Industry experience		
Managing the assignment, e.g. • Co-ordination and leadership • Quality processes • Fee management • Balance of senior/junior time • Continuity		
Wider resources and credentials, e.g. • Depth and breadth of expertise • Geographical coverage • Existing credibility with the client • Firm's general reputation		

This may influence the inflection you give to a win theme, or whether you choose it as one of your key messages. For example, you might be more inclined to emphasise local service if you know that you are the only firm with an office close to theirs; or your experience in a particular type of transaction, if your track record in the field is more extensive than the competition.

You should recognise the limitations of trying to analyse competitors in this context. For a start, you may not find out who they are. Even if you do, it can be difficult to second-guess how a competitor may respond to a particular opportunity. It may depend on who is leading the team. Law firms may be much more corporate than they used to be, but there is still scope for individuals to stamp their imprimatur on the exercise.

More fundamentally, corporate legal advice is a mature industry in which buyers are usually able to choose between a number of prospective service providers with very similar resources, capabilities and track record. It will not often be the case that you can claim clear differentiation in these areas.

Instead you should seek to distinguish yourself through factors relating to the particular circumstances of the tender. This can be done for example by showing sensitivity to the client's particular concerns; choosing a team which precisely matches its requirements; and quantifying the benefits that will be gained through your approach.

Competitor analysis can of course be applied to the financial as well as the technical part of the proposal. This is addressed later in the chapter.

Reflecting the organisation's values

Win themes are generally expressed as business benefits that the target organisation will gain from the firm's involvement. But an increasingly important aspect of creating a winning narrative is also to demonstrate affinity with the organisation's values and ethical commitments.

Firms therefore need to think about how their conduct of the proposal may be interpreted by decision-makers. Areas which warrant specific attention are diversity and inclusiveness as well as corporate social responsibility (CSR). Many private as well as public sector organisations favour suppliers which can show they take a pro-active approach to promoting equal opportunities. The most visible sign of what is likely to be the firm's attitude in this area is the choice of staff it selects for the proposal team. Diversity may therefore need to be on the agenda from the early stages of planning the bid.

Bid teams should be aware of the organisation's CSR priorities and where possible draw parallels between these and its own pro bono and community initiatives. It is noteworthy that legislative changes (such as the new EU procurement directives) are encouraging public sector contracting authorities to build social value into their award criteria, alongside the technical and financial evaluation.

The anatomy of persuasion

A major part of a lawyer's job is to be persuasive, and members of the profession are familiar with how to put together a convincing argument. But skills practised in working with clients on legal issues do not always translate to business development or tendering.

It is helpful to return to one to the original and still definitive formulations of the elements involved in creating a persuasive case, as proposed by Aristotle. He identified three means of appealing to an audience:

Logos is an appeal to logic, and is a way of persuading an audience by reason.

Pathos is an appeal to emotion, and is intended to convince by creating an emotional response.

Ethos is an appeal to ethics, and is a means of convincing the reader or listener of the character or credibility of the persuader.

These appeals have direct parallels with the ingredients we need to include if we are to persuade potential buyers to select us. We should add to this a fourth element. Presumably in debates in the agora, speakers did not need to justify why they were addressing the topic at hand. In a tender, however, we need to explain to or remind the recipient why this topic matters and has consequences for the organisation. In other words, we should highlight what the 'issue' is. This is the first element to be addressed in constructing a persuasive message.

Issue

Citing a subject that is of importance to the evaluators is the first step in getting their attention. It could be, for example, a compliance risk, management problem, practical obstacle or commercial opportunity. An issue arises out of and reflects the evaluators' perception of the organisation's needs. The extent to which you have to explain it will depend on the context. For example, you will be able to write or say less if you know the readers are already aware of the matter. A more detailed explanation may be required if you are bringing it to their attention for the first time.

Solution

This is the second element - the descendant of logos, the appeal to reason. This is the course of action you are suggesting to address the issue you have highlighted. In a tender, it is what you are proposing to do if you are selected.

Benefit

The equivalent of pathos – or more precisely, an appeal to reason and emotion in combination. You articulate how the reader will gain from taking the action you have suggested. The solution describes what you are going to do; the benefit describes the favourable outcomes that will result. The more specific and quantifiable the benefit described, the more impact it is likely to have.

Evidence

Evidence is the counterpart of ethos. You need to provide evidence to support your claim that the solution you have proposed will be effective. This will include demonstrating that your firm has the experience, track record, resources and wherewithal to deliver.

The way you set out these points will not always be the same. On occasion there may be an overlap, so that you do not need to address all of them separately. But you should feel that these four 'bases' have been covered, at least implicitly.

In planning your tender response, it may be helpful to use a grid to outline what you think the key issues facing the client are; and, in each case, what your approach is going to be, how the client will gain from this and why you are the right team to be appointed:

Issues	Solutions	Benefits	Evidence

The issues, solutions, benefits, and evidence (ISBE) approach is perhaps best illustrated by a case study. The following is based on an actual new business opportunity faced by a medium sized UK firm.

Case study

> The situation: one of the firm's corporate & commercial partners was invited to a meeting with the general secretary of a major trade association operating within the transport sector. Also in attendance was the association's head of legal services (one of a two-person in-house legal team). The association's purpose was to provide support to its members, which varied from one-man bands to medium sized companies.

> The general secretary explained that the association had been suffering declining membership for some years, a fact he attributed to a failure to refresh the package of benefits provided to members. Principal among these was a legal helpline, providing advice to callers on topics ranging from compliance with industry regulations to employee and commercial disputes. The general secretary said that the helpline was phone-only; he felt that members required a more sophisticated offering, including an on-line portal providing more detailed guidance than would be available from a short phone call. He also felt that this should be supported by other initiatives, such as sending email alerts or setting up a programme of seminars on topical legal issues affecting the industry.

> Although the management team received details of the number and duration of calls received via the helpline each month, this did not include a detailed breakdown of the topics covered. It was therefore difficult to monitor trends in membership needs – information that could be helpful in refining the package for existing members and marketing to new ones.

> The head of legal said that, with a view to controlling legal costs, it would be helpful if the successful firm could provide support and knowledge-sharing so that a wider range of matters could be handled by the in-house team.

> The general secretary observed that the association's existing legal advisers were a small firm with which he had a long-standing personal connection. The current service made no provision for

review meetings and he had found it difficult to convey his misgivings about what was currently being offered both to members and the association's legal team.

The partner returned to the office and thought about what his firm should offer the association in the light of this meeting. His conclusions were reflected in the one-page summary to the proposal document, set out over the page.

First draft

We have summarised below the range of benefits that we can offer to the association and its members:

Key client review meetings	We would propose our first review meeting three months after being selected. We would then suggest regular review meetings with our Relationship Partner to discuss performance and other matters. In addition to the above, our business development team conducts biennial face-to-face interviews with our key clients to ensure that we continue to meet their requirements and to identify any areas where there might be room for improvement. We use this continuous improvement process as an opportunity to listen to the client's views on the quality and extent of the service that we provide.
Bespoke training workshops	As a full service firm we can offer a range of workshops tailored to the business needs of the association and its members.
Extranet/Case Management System	We can offer the association and its members a case management system which is not only tailored to their particular requirements but which has the important advantage of enabling them to view all documents produced or obtained by us. We offer this real time extranet facility free of charge.
Provision of secondees	Subject to agreeing terms, we may be able to offer a secondee to attend the association's offices or the offices of one of its members. This is something we have supplied to clients previously and we would be happy to discuss the options with you.
Newsletters	We produce a range of newsletters and alerts to ensure you are kept up to date with legal developments.
Additional seminars	We offer our clients and contacts the opportunity to attend seminars across a range of legal disciplines including corporate, commercial, IP and IT, employment, commercial property and tax.

The offers in the first draft are perhaps not the most imaginative, but the partner has done what he thought was necessary to respond to the issues raised in the meeting. In spite of this, the text does not suggest the author is thinking about the client's particular circumstances and concerns.

The overall impression created by this draft is that the firm has a number of things that it can offer, but appears less concerned about the context in which they will be delivered or how they will further the client's objectives. This impression is reinforced by the lack of specific examples of what it has done elsewhere that are relevant to this particular client.

Given the emphasis which clients put on the importance of having advisers who understand their business and sector, we should conclude that the answers are not showing the firm in the best light.

The raw material in the second draft (over the page) is not fundamentally different from that in the first; but it is likely to have much more impact on the reader. This is because a reference to issue, solution, benefit and evidence is integrated into each point. For example, the text in the right had column starts with a reference to what the organisation wants to achieve, or what it is concerned about. (The only exception is the final point, where it would be indelicate to refer to the incumbent's failure to communicate effectively).

Whereas the headings set out in the left hand column in the first draft itemise the actions it is proposing to take, the revised headings in the second draft paint a picture of how the organisation will gain through these actions. The examples of work done for other clients is more specific and relevant, strengthening the ethos part of the persuasion framework.

Having identified the issues which matter to this prospective client, the author of the second draft has also ordered them effectively. It must be right to start with the impact the legal service will have on attracting and retaining members – surely likely to be the general secretary's primary concern.

Second draft

Meeting your objectives

Helping you to increase membership	One of the association's primary objectives is to reverse the trend in falling membership. We intend to play a full part in increasing the perceived value of the association among existing members and potential recruits. For example we will send members email alerts on legal developments affecting their businesses, encompassing both industry-specific and general commercial issues. Members will also be invited to attend our monthly programme of seminars, which feature external experts as well as our own specialists. Recent topics have included litigation trends in transport and logistics, how SMEs can ensure their IP protection is cost effective and avoiding employee discrimination claims.
Information shared - instantly	We understand that members have had difficulty getting up to date information on cases affecting them. All members and authorised users will have access to all case details in real time, through a dedicated portal. We now provide a bespoke extranet to over a dozen membership organisations, in all cases with positive results. "Your Extranet has helped to transform day to day communications for members." Dave X, secretary general, XYZ.
Building your in-house legal skills	You wish to broaden the skills base of you in-house team. One way we can share our skills is by providing a part-time secondee. We will also invite your staff to spend time at our offices, as part of the learning process. At one of our clients, our secondment programme has been reported to have led to a substantial increase in productivity in the department.
Staying in tune with what you want	In addition to regular meetings with the service team, we would like periodically to carry out an independent review of our relationship with the association. This would normally take the form of face of face interviews with your key personnel, conducted by a senior member of the firm who is unconnected with service delivery. In our experience the review process is invaluable in identifying issues which do not always emerge in the day-to-day relationship. It provides an additional opportunity for us to assess how we can improve our performance and anticipate your evolving requirements.

As with the win themes discussed at the beginning of this chapter, you are trying to tie what you are proposing to do with what we believe the client needs:

The Prospective Client	Your Firm
Issues	Solutions
Benefits	Evidence

The key to building a rounded, persuasive argument is to create a balance between the four elements in the ISBE framework. Where this balance is lacking, the case put forward is unlikely to convince.

For example, dwelling on the issues facing the organisation at the expense of the other elements may show that you have a good understanding of it. But without proposing solutions, the firm will appear in a passive light. Understanding the client is a means to an end, not an end in itself.

The solutions-orientated message (as in the first version of the case study text) suggests that we would have proposed the same thing for any client. We are more concerned about selling what we can do than adapting our skills to meeting an individual need.

Words which convey benefits without describing solutions and evidence may paint a rosy picture, but they will lack credibility; how will this better future be achieved, and why is this firm the best one to deliver it?

Like the issues-oriented message, evidence-only text is passive. However, in this case we are likely to make even less of an impression, as we are talking about our own organisation rather than the reader's. Credentials and capability statements fall into this category. They may be frequently requested; but their ability to advance the firm's cause will always be limited.

Though particularly relevant to tenders and new business proposals, the framework can be applied to almost any medium where you are seeking to persuade - whether website, newsletter, client report or internal memo.

Engaging with procurement

So far we have looked at bid strategy primarily in the context of persuading the primary decisions makers – typically senior members of the in-house legal team or central and operational management. While the tender is in progress, however, bidders' sole dialogue with the organisation may be with the procurement contact. Your bid strategy hence also needs to address your approach with procurement.

Some aspects of liaising with procurement are outlined in chapter 3, such as the approach you might take to seeking clarifications having analysed the RFP. Another common issue is how to respond where there are mistakes or anomalies in the tender documentation. Some firms are reluctant to raise questions about them, for fear of alienating the authors.

In both the public and private sectors, bidders should actively engage with procurement teams and be willing to question aspects of the process if they believe them to be flawed – provided it is done in a constructive fashion. As suggested in chapter 1, bidders that try to influence the tender process often do better than those which merely seek to comply with it.

As with many other corporate activities, procurement departments are often under pressure to demonstrate that they are capable of identifying and implementing continuous improvement; feedback from current and prospective suppliers is therefore important to them. In the words of one consultant who advises public sector procurement departments:

> "Bidders tend to be too passive – they worry that if they question the process they will jeopardise their chances. That's simply not the case."

With an increasing number of public sector contract awards being subject to legal challenge by disgruntled bidders, procurement departments within government bodies are conscious of the need to be seen to be following fair and best practice. But this increasingly applies to other types of organisations which have a procurement function.

Even where advised that access to operational decision-makers will be restricted, it is worth explaining why a meeting with the relevant people will help you submit a better bid. This may lead to a change of approach. (If this happens, though, it is very likely that all bidders will be invited to engage in the same way – a factor you may wish to take into account before making the request).

Being proactive about the tender process should not be mistaken for ignoring instructions or trying to circumvent the procurement department.

Part of the bidder's aim should be to understand procurement's role. If possible, try to make the department look good within its organisation. Even where the procurement professionals appear to lack influence, it is a mistake to alienate them:

> "The procurement department can be your best friend or your worst enemy - developing a dialogue will serve you very well."
> (Procurement director, financial services)

> "Take advantage of opportunities to speak by phone with procurement staff. Clarifying information can be useful in crafting a more responsive proposal." (Sourcing manager, legal services, insurance industry)

As with other types of buyers, the most effective way to work with procurement is to have already built a relationship with the individuals outside the tender period. Incumbent advisers clearly have an advantage in this respect. The next section addresses the question of how incumbents can capitalise on the existing relationship – while avoiding the pitfalls which go with being in this position.

Notes for re-bidders

Private sector organisations increasingly choose to review their suppliers regularly, typically in a two to four year timeframe, for governance reasons. Public bodies are obliged to do so by law. So finding ways to improve the firm's prospects of getting reappointed has become a critical part of client management.

Assuming the relationship has not broken down, incumbents usually start the tender process with some powerful advantages. For the client, sticking with the devil you know is often the lowest risk and cost option. The incumbent firm should have a better understanding of the organisation's strategic priorities - and of the contract itself - than outsiders. It has the credibility that goes with experience of the day-to-day realities of delivering the service. In view of this, it is not surprising that incumbents win a large proportion of re-bids – in the range of 40 to 60 per cent in most sectors.

On the other hand, incumbents also have their vulnerabilities. Buyer surveys suggest that incumbent bidders' biggest enemy can often be their own complacency. (See for example *Attitudes to Incumbents*, Rebidding

Solutions, 2013). Too many firms, it seems, simply assume they will be reappointed and approach the tender as 'business as usual'.

> "Incumbents should offer new added-value features, improved or creative pricing, or both. Decision-makers may view a failure to do so as complacency on their part, especially where improved pricing or value-added services are stated explicitly as desired outcomes of the process." (Sourcing manager, legal services, insurance industry)

What's more, some buyers believe that a fresh perspective brings inherent benefits, whether they feel the incumbent is doing a good job or not. Changes in the client's management team are often a prelude to a shake up among advisers.

The growing influence of procurement departments and procurement thinking can be a threat to incumbents. As discussed in chapter 1, procurement professionals often see their role in terms of bringing greater objectivity to the purchasing decision. They are interested in measuring the outputs and outcomes firms have achieved (or say they will achieve).

Procurement is also typically suspicious of what they might regard as "cosy" relationships between end-users and their suppliers. Consequently, RFPs increasingly include questions on how firms will add value, create innovation and achieve continuous improvement.

Evaluators in the public sector are not allowed to take account of the general relationship with an incumbent (or indeed anything else which cannot be put in the submission and supported with evidence). Such thinking is increasingly prevalent in the private sector. For the purposes of the tender, these clients will treat their current advisers in exactly the same way as other bidders. The existing relationship may count for nothing - unless the incumbent can find a way to show in its tender response that previous achievements are relevant to the new contract.

In light of these developments, how can incumbents maximise their chances of being re-appointed? The first requirement is to make sure your client is satisfied with your firm's work on the existing contract. An unfavourable opinion of the firm, especially when held by senior management within the organisation, is very likely to be reflected in the outcome - despite affirmations that all contenders start the competition on an equal footing.

Secondly, recognise that a tender signifies change in some form; not necessarily to the firms chosen to do the work, but certainly to some aspects of how the engagement will be conducted.

This may be difficult for some fee-earners to accept: if they have been doing excellent work, it should be enough to promise to continue in the same vein. But this is to misunderstand the psychology of the buyer. Whether those launching the tender are complying with a mandatory requirement or motivated by broader governance considerations, they will want to see a return on the investment of time and effort that the organisation has to put into the process. So even if the firm has an impeccable track record with the organisation, incumbents must use the tender as an opportunity to introduce improvements. It may be very difficult, however, to work out what these ought to be without a lot of preparation in advance of the tender.

Firms should start planning for the rebid at the beginning of the initial contract period. There are five areas in particular which may need to be kept in mind for the whole duration of the contract:

Succession planning

Particularly in connection with long-term engagements, re-bidders tend to emphasise the value of continuity in avoiding disruption, maximising efficiency and mitigating risk. At the same time, they are aware that firms that have not worked with the organisation before have novelty value and will claim to be able to offer the organisation a fresh perspective.

One way incumbents can counter this is by offering some novelty of their own. A frequently used method is to introduce new people to the team. At the time of winning the original instruction, the lead or client relationship partner needs to think about how the team should evolve during the lifetime of the contract and what its composition is likely to be when the service is re-tendered. Preferably new faces will have been introduced some time before then, giving them the opportunity to start building a rapport with decision-makers.

Potential added value features

Possible innovations which could be proposed in the next tender should be kept under review as the contract progresses. These might include training in an area which has not been covered before; proposing a change to processes involving the taking of instructions or reporting on the status of current matters; or providing templates which will enable the client to carry out more work in-house.

Client feedback and performance planning

On most assignments the service team will have an opportunity to discuss the progress of the engagement with the client, making adjustments as necessary where the team's approach can be refined. While this may be a routine aspect of client management, its potential importance to the next tender is often overlooked. The service team needs to keep a close track of changes it introduces during the contract, as this may provide valuable evidence of its commitment to and capacity for continuous improvement (see also below).

The independent client service review adds an extra dimension in this respect. Typically this should involve face-to-face interviews with key users of the service. The interviews should be held around the middle-point of the contract (or in some cases annually) and conducted by a consultant or a senior member of the firm who has no connection with the delivery of the service. The main purpose of the interviews is to:

- Take stock of the overall relationship

- Refine the firm's understanding of what the organisation is looking for from its external legal advisers

- Identify potential issues which may not have surfaced during the course of the day to day relationship

- Identify and discuss potential improvements to the service

- Develop a stronger understanding of how the organisation's needs are likely to evolve; and of what the implications of this will be for the future provision of the service

The interview phase would be followed by internal discussion and the development of a plan detailing improvement initiatives, to be subsequently agreed with the client. The client service review needs to take place sufficiently in advance of the next tender to allow time for improvement initiatives to be at least partially implemented.

Developing long term relationships with procurement

Firms should aim to understand and influence the client's buying process. That might include: being aware of the trigger for the requirement and conditioning the buyers to the firm's capabilities before the proposal starts; understanding the tools they use and how they are going to evaluate the bids; making it easy for the procurement team to sell your firm internally; and planning for negotiation during rather than after the proposal phase.

The need to target individuals and develop relationships over time is as important with procurement professionals as with any other type of client. A potential role for bid and business development specialists is to create a dialogue with procurement officers. They are in many respects natural counterparts, as fee-earners and in-house counsel are. Business development should aim to create a continuing relationship, as procurement officers are likely to be far more receptive to external influences between tender events than when they are in progress.

This dialogue might focus on management issues such as refining the means by which external firms' performance can be measured; developing new ways of sharing knowhow with the in-house legal team; organising independent client service or 360° reviews; and increasing value from existing legal spend. Helping to shape procurement's thinking on these issues may enable the firm to gain significant advantages - for example by ensuring that the specifications and award criteria in the next tender play to the firm's strengths.

> "Seek to influence other procurement activities, not just the proposal." (Procurement director, IT industry)

Collecting evidence of achievements

While tender responses must be predominantly forward looking – what the firm intends to do in the future, not what it has done over the last contract period – incumbents should take the opportunity to remind decision-makers of the tangible outputs and benefits that have been achieved throughout the contract. These are easily forgotten after the event. So the team should adopt a system of logging helpful evidence, including any favourable comments received at the time from people within the organisation.

It is becoming increasingly common for corporate clients to include a performance-related element in the fee arrangements they agree with their firms. Criteria which may be used to adjust the level of fees include commercial outcomes (where these can be measured), average response times and the accuracy of estimating the legal costs of individual matters. Such metrics can be used in the next tender to remind the client of the firm's strong performance.

Material of this kind should help you score points in the rebid. Some care is required in how you present it in the document, however, because of the danger of appearing to have a 'business as usual' attitude. Details of accomplishments to date are often most persuasive when presented as a step towards increasing the value of the service further in the next contract period.

Pricing

The financial crisis, increasing influence of procurement, developments in outsourcing and offshoring, alternative business structures, and demand for more value-based charging have all contributed to a climate where firms are expected to keep cutting their fees. That is before taking into account the possible impact of technology on how certain types of work are done and charged for.

In spite of these changes, approaches to identifying how to pitch the price on a particular tender have not changed fundamentally over the years. Mechanisms such as capped fees, blended rates, price locks and remuneration linked to outcomes have become more common, but firms do not always think systematically about the level of fee which is likely to give them a competitive advantage.

Teams have tended to put all the effort into developing a proposal that they hope will appeal to the decision-makers. With the deadline approaching, somebody will calculate how much it is going to cost to deliver the service; then a group of senior partners takes a view on the level of the profit that can be built in without scaring off the prospect. However, the traditional 'cost plus' approach to pricing is being increasingly challenged.

Price-to-Win (PTW) is a way of thinking about bids which is transforming the competitive landscape. PTW has been primarily adopted by companies bidding for large contracts in defence, IT and outsourcing sectors. However, it is increasingly used in professional services, for example by the major accountants and management consultancies. There is no reason why it should not be embraced by law firms and other legal services providers, especially if they are involved in major bids.

The method involves in-depth competitor analysis, including pricing estimates based on competitors' past performance and likely approach to the solution. A cost-driven marketplace demands that solutions are determined by a clear conception of what the winning price is going to be – not the other way round. Bidders have to align their approach with this reality.

PTW can lead to radical changes in the management of the proposal process. A common technique is the appointment of a 'black hat' team to second-guess competitors' pricing strategy. Another critical element is encouraging 'intrepreneurship', by setting work-streams a price target and incentivising them to undershoot it.

A further implication – one which may not be entirely comfortable for people who have spent years acquiring proposal skills – is that firms need to adjust the way they allocate bid resources. One suggestion is that they should spend at least 10 per cent of the overall budget on competitor analysis (currently mostly zero per cent) and that strategic pricing should get a similar allocation (up from 5 per cent). The proportion of resources devoted to the range of activities normally associated with proposal development should fall from around 60 per cent to 45 per cent or less.

All of which suggests that pricing strategists will play an increasingly prominent role in the bid departments of tomorrow.

The pricing of legal work is a subject in itself. Books on this topic include:

> Ronald J. Baker, Implementing Value Pricing: A Radical Business Model for Professional Firms (2010)
> Toby Brown and Vincent Cordo, Law Firm Pricing: Strategies, Roles, and Responsibilities (2013)
> Stuart Dodds, Smarter Pricing, Smarter Profit: A Guide for the Law Firm of the Future (2017)
> Patrick Lamb, Alternative Fee Arrangements: Value Fees and the Changing Legal Market (2013)
> Jim Hassett, Legal Project Management, Pricing, and Alternative Fee Arrangements (2013)

Chapter 5 at a glance:
Developing the Bid Strategy

Win themes

A win theme is an articulation of why you are the right firm to be chosen for the assignment or role that has been put out to tender. It should encapsulate both a need which you have identified as being important to the prospective client, and evidence that you are able to satisfy that need. You should be able to express it in a sentence or short paragraph. In selecting win themes, where possible you should take into account competitors' ability to satisfy the needs you have identified.

The anatomy of persuasion

Whether through the written or spoken word, persuasive arguments tend to combine four elements. You need to get the evaluators' attention by showing that you are addressing something important to them; propose a course of action which addresses the issue you have raised; articulate how this solution will lead to benefits for the organisation; and then provide evidence that you have the capability to deliver the solution.

Engaging with procurement

Bidders should actively engage with procurement teams and be willing to question aspects of the process if they believe them to be flawed – provided it is done in a constructive and unthreatening fashion. Trying to reach the ultimate decision-makers by circumventing the procurement function is almost certain to backfire. The most effective way to influence procurement departments is to build a relationship with them over the long term.

Notes for re-bidders

Regardless of how well the firm has performed on the existing contract, the team needs to demonstrate its capacity to embrace continuous improvement. This requires long-term planning – incumbents need to start preparing for the next tender as soon as they start work on the contract. For example a succession plan, unfolding during the lifetime of the contract, will often enable the firm to show that it is introducing fresh blood to the relationship while continuing to offer the benefits of continuity.

A client service review mid-way through the contract can be a highly effective means of identifying areas where the service can be improved – and should allow enough time for improvement initiatives to be implemented. This will provide material which can be turned into helpful narrative in the next tender submission.

Pricing

Although fee levels are under pressure as never before, approaches to pricing have not changed fundamentally over the years. Firms should consider incorporating Price-To-Win techniques into their approach to bidding – a method based on the premise that, in industry generally, the majority of contracts are won by the lowest priced bidder meeting an acceptable standard.

6. The Submission

Context
The free-form proposal
Questionnaires
Visual style
Tools and templates
Reviewing and improving the draft
Roles in producing the submission
eProcurement
New formats

Context

Nearly all competitive proposals involve the submission of some form of documentation – although that can range from a brief email to hundreds of pages of text. While much of this chapter focuses on the requirements associated with more formal tenders, many of the principles can be applied to any selection process.

One of the clearest distinctions between the traditional type of proposal and the procurement-driven evaluation (see chapter 1) is the difference in attitude and approach to the written word.

The type 1 submission

In a type 1 tender, the document is likely to be more a means of gathering information about the contenders than deciding which ones to choose. That is particularly the case with the variety of submission known as the credentials or capability statement. Arguably these are not really proposals at all, as they do not ask you what you are going to do or how the firm will go about tackling an assignment or set of instructions.

Even where the contenders are asked to include material more specific to the client or the requirement, the document in a type 1 tender is often used mainly to compare fees, check capabilities and decide which firms to invite to the presentation stage.

This is not to imply that the document in this type of competition is irrelevant to the outcome. It is often said that 'proposal documents cannot win the tender but they can lose it'. In other words, the written submission is unlikely to be decisive in the final selection but it has the power to damage your credibility if it is perceived to be sub-standard.

It is also likely to be important in helping the service team to focus on developing key messages and the main themes of the proposal, including why you believe you are the right firm to be selected. This material will be relevant to the presentation.

By the end of the process, however, decision-makers have often forgotten what was in the document. This is confirmed by debriefing discussions, at which they will often vividly recall details of the presentations but only have the vaguest recollection of which firm said what in their submission.

The type 2 submission

In type 2 tenders the written word is much more significant. As discussed in chapter 1, the aim of the type 2 tender exercise is to form at least a partially objective assessment of which firms are right for the organisation rather than merely to identify which the users of the service prefer.

Procurement departments tend to attach importance to the written word, and promote its role within the assessment process, because the submission is more susceptible to scrutiny and review than a presentation. Unless recorded, the presentation disappears into the ether once the meeting is over. The tender responses will be scored according to specific criteria, shared with the contenders in advance. Being able to show that the organisation has followed an auditable and transparent process plays to the procurement department's objectivity agenda.

Bidders are usually required to submit written information either by producing a free-form proposal or completing a questionnaire. The former is strongly associated with type 1 tenders, the latter with type 2; although exceptions are not infrequent.

The free-form proposal

Some RFPs specify a number of topics to which bidders are asked to respond, while leaving the structure of the document up to the respondent. In these circumstances, there are two key principles to bear in mind when considering how to order the material. Content which is explicitly tailored to the prospective client will have much more impact than general 'boilerplate'; and the front of the document is more likely to be read thoroughly than the middle or the back.

Taking these two points together, it makes sense to ensure that the key messages you want to convey to the decision-makers – together with commentary which is specific to their organisation – should be given a prominent position. So should the details on your team: their assessment of the individuals you have chosen to put forward for the engagement will be highly influential in determining the outcome.

Sections on process and methodology should usually come afterwards, together with the fee proposal and a more general description of the firm's overall resources and credentials.

The logic behind how the material is ordered should be evident to the reader. A key principle is to deal with topics one at a time, and in one place only. Legal proposals often fail to do this. It means not diluting the force of one point or advantage you are able to offer by mixing it up with another which is unrelated to it.

On the other hand, the material will be easier to assimilate if you emphasise the linkages between topics which are related and deal with them in the same part of the proposal. Usually the document should therefore contain relatively few sections, each devoted to covering a 'family' of points. By the same token, avoid repeating the same point in different parts of the document (unless you want to refer to it in the summary).

The structure of the submission will depend on the circumstances and the material at your disposal, but a possible outline is as follows:

Summary

Meeting your objectives

Our team

Managing the engagement

Fees

About the firm

Summary

The purpose of the summary is not to provide a microcosm of everything that is in the proposal: instead, it should make the case for why the firm should be selected. Every proposal should include a summary of this kind unless the specification explicitly instructs you to omit it.

Usually the summary should be kept to one page. Apart from a short introduction and conclusion, it should highlight three or four reasons why you believe yours is the right firm for the assignment. Each should be given its own paragraph. Each should start with a sentence, not more than one line, which itself summarises the point. This opening sentence can be visually emphasised, for example by using bold print.

The reasons you put forward should highlight the firm's main attributes (and differentiators if it has them) - but should be linked to the main outcomes you think the organisation wishes to achieve as a result of the procurement. Thus the benefits of appointing the firm must come across clearly. The second draft of the sample summary in in chapter 5 is an illustration of this approach.

The summary can take the form of a cover letter. This may be particularly appropriate in tenders which have a more personal dimension - where for example the tender is addressed to a named recipient who has worked with or otherwise has some connection with the team.

As with any summary, the cover letter is an integral part of the proposal and should (in a hard copy submission) be bound into the document. In a free-form proposal, it should be the first thing the reader sees – and placed therefore before the table of contents.

Meeting your objectives

The opening section is the one which is likely to have the most impact and be the best read (apart from the fee proposal!). It should include the material which is most likely to interest the decision-makers, such as what you can do to enhance their business or help them achieve their aims. This might involve you in for example minimising risks, improving the use of resources, sharing knowhow or speeding up the legal processes involved in delivering operational objectives.

The heading for the section should get this theme across - 'Meeting your objectives' is one possibility; 'Supporting [ABC's] development' or 'Helping you to deliver XYZ' (referring to the project you are bidding for) are others. This section must be highly tailored to the prospective client's circumstances and should not include standard boilerplate on the firm. Drawing on past experience of working with the organisation, personal contacts with the management team or desk research, this section should aim to:

- Show that you have understood the issues and concerns facing the decision-makers

- Demonstrate that you are capable of developing practical solutions to address these issues

- Articulate clearly how the organisation will benefit from your firm's involvement

- Substantiate your claims with evidence or examples

In other words, it should use the ISBE approach as described in chapter 5. You might consider introducing this with one or two paragraphs which sum up the stage of development the organisation has reached, perhaps referring to the management (or legal) team's achievements but also highlighting the challenges it faces. This will create a platform for you to discuss the key issues and how you will help the organisation to address them. The quality of the document as a whole, and this section in particular, will often depend on how well your team has understood the issues facing the organisation.

Our team

The team section should introduce or remind the decision-makers of the key individuals you are putting forward, the role they will play on the engagement and why they are well qualified to carry out these roles effectively.

Define the roles of each team member as well as highlighting their experience. Segregate this material in some way, for example by covering the individual's role and experience in separate paragraphs

Make sure that the description of the roles underpins the messages you want to get across about how the service will be delivered. For example, if you know the prospective client wants to use legal advisers as a sounding board on broader issues, be sure to mention this in describing the role of the team leader. If the decision-makers are worried about the disruption that a project will cause, or turnover of staff on the engagement, you may want to say that maximising continuity and effective scheduling of the work will be key parts of the team leader/project manager's role.

The biographies should be kept short (perhaps two to three paragraphs) and should focus on the individuals' most recent and relevant client experience, rather than providing chapter and verse on their careers, when and where they qualified, what positions they hold within the firm and where they went to school. This of course tends to be much easier where the team is dedicated to a specialist sector. Where possible, refer to clients; if for reasons of confidentiality that is not possible, describe the type of organisation and the work done without naming them.

Managing the engagement

There is often a requirement for a section in the document which outlines your methodologies and covers the mechanics of service delivery. As with the opening section you need to explain how the organisation will gain from your approach. The emphasis here though is likely to be on demonstrating how you will deliver the service efficiently rather than on your ability to add value or bring wider business benefits to the organisation. Some of the areas you may want to cover in this section include:

- Process, methodology and timetable
- Communication and reporting

- Quality assurance procedures

- Key performance indicators (KPIs)

- Service team continuity and succession

- Managing potential conflicts

The section should normally be kept fairly brief. Some of the material, such as descriptions of processes or a project timetable, may be best presented using charts (see 'Visual style' below).

Fees

In setting out the fee, be sure to give enough information about your approach to pricing to ensure that the recipients understand your reasoning and the thought that went into it. The fee should also remind the reader of any value-added features which are to be included in the price.

About the firm

The purpose of the final section is to reinforce the earlier material by showing that the firm has the overall resources, infrastructure and credentials to provide the back-up and support which the service team may need to carry out the assignment effectively. Topics you should consider for this section include the firm's structure and brief statistics on people and offices; client list; examples of relevant assignments; and additional services.

Appendices

By putting material in an appendix, you are effectively giving it the status of an 'optional extra' which is to be considered at the reader's discretion. In practice that is an invitation not to read it. As a rule of thumb, only generic material should be put in an appendix – standard CVs, pro-formas, templates etc. Generic material usually contributes little to a proposal and indeed may be negatively received. So it follows that appendices should usually be kept to a minimum.

Do not put information which has a direct bearing on your bid in an appendix. This includes profiles of team members which highlights relevant experience to the assignment or client. At best, this will cause the reader the inconvenience of having to refer to the back of the document while reading the main body.

Indexing

In the free-form response the authors are at liberty to order the material so that it has maximum impact. They may, however, be concerned that adopting their own structure will make it less easy for the recipients to find answers to the requests for information set out in the invitation letter or document. This will particularly be the case where the RFP includes a long or detailed list of questions.

You can get round this problem by including a response matrix or index, which matches each of the points requiring a response in the RFP with a page reference. The index should be prominently placed within the document – perhaps on the inside front cover (opposite the letter), or on the same page as or immediately after the table of contents.

Questionnaires

The questionnaire has become the standard method for evaluating tender responses for public sector and institutional clients at both pre-qualification and RFP stages. (There are moves afoot in the government sector, incidentally, to simplify or replace PQQs as part of a continuing effort to make it easier for SMEs to participate in public procurements. For example, in the UK the PQQ has been replaced by the self-certifying selection questionnaire. Private sector organisations may follow this example.)

The questionnaire format is favoured because contracting organisations (and particularly their procurement departments) believe it facilitates comparison between bids and leads to greater consistency in evaluation.

While bidders obviously have much less discretion in how they order their material, many principles and suggestions relating to free-form documents still apply. For example, although it is not always obvious where to put it, a summary or key messages statement of some kind should be included wherever possible. Even if it is not officially scored by the evaluators, it will set the tone for the rest of the document and may provide the only opportunity for the firm to get across the case for being chosen in condensed form. In fact, procurement professionals typically recommend that firms include a summary, unless specifically instructed not to do so.

When responding to questionnaires, it is particularly important to understand how reviewers will evaluate the document. For example, the weighting of the questions needs to be taken into account in considering how much detail to provide. It is increasingly common for procurement professionals to stipulate a word or character-limit for some or all of the answers. Where these are not provided, as a rule of thumb authors should aim to ensure that the amount of text provided is in proportion to the weighting.

If in doubt, find out if separate sections will be scored by the same or different evaluators. This can have a bearing on, for example, whether you should cross-refer between sections or reproduce answers where questions appear to overlap.

Answering the question

According to procurement professionals, the most frequently recurring mistake tenderers commit is 'failing to answer the question'. This may occur because of a natural tendency to address the question the author wanted to answer, rather than the question actually asked. Or because the answer has been borrowed from another tender response, where the question was not quite the same. On the other hand, some questions may be badly worded or ambiguous, and therefore difficult to interpret. In the case of all but the most routine questions, it pays to invest time up front understanding what the questioner had in mind before starting to write.

Getting to the point

You need to show the evaluator that you are answering the question as quickly as possible. You also need to get across the essence of your message before the evaluator has a chance to get distracted or lose concentration.

Therefore, do not begin with preamble or introduction. The first paragraph should summarise your whole answer, bringing to the reader's attention the key points you want to get across. Also bear in mind that your emphasis should be on what you are proposing to do, rather than what you think your general characteristics, philosophies or aspirations are – the latter is almost impossible to evaluate or give a mark for.

The importance of evidence

The evaluators will have been tasked with making an independent assessment of the tender responses. That means they should not take into account any factors which are extraneous to the tender response itself (such as the firm's reputation, existing relationships with the organisation or how the firm is currently regarded by users of the service).

The answers therefore need to be self-sufficient and able to be assessed on their own merits. Any claims that the firm makes on its own behalf must be supported with verifiable evidence. The evaluators may not be familiar with the firm; they may have no direct experience of using the service. You need to provide them with material which enables them to form a judgement about your ability to meet the organisation's needs:

As with free-form documents, anything that substantively contributes to the proposal should be in the body of the answer - not relegated to an appendix.

Demonstrating understanding of the client organisation

Again in common with free-form proposals, the key to maximising your score is to show how you will apply the firm's experience, resources, expertise and approach in the context of the client's specific circumstances and objectives; and how you will use your understanding of the client to achieve the best outcomes. Use the ISBE method (see chapter 5) wherever possible in responding to individual questions.

Visual style

Appearances matter – although the extent to which they do will depend on the nature of the tender and type of recipient. Some decision-makers are happy to admit that the visual style of document can make as much of an impression on them as the content. But even evaluators who focus all their energies on the latter are likely to be affected subliminally by how the information is presented.

In many tendering exercises the scope for firms to apply visual devices or motifs to their submission is restricted. In extreme cases (as quite often happens where the document is to be submitted through an on-line portal) no images will be permitted; the procurement professional may even specify the size and type of font that has to be used. Even in these situations, authors have the opportunity to influence the reader by laying out the text in a way that aids comprehension and supports the content.

Laying out the page

Use layout to convey a sense of order and to help the reader to see at a glance the ground that you are covering in a section or answer. This will help the evaluator to absorb your approach to tackling the issue at hand and that you are covering all the relevant points.

The most commonly used layout device is the bullet point. Many authors think this is a good way of breaking up the text. But note that bullet points, especially in an extended list, do not help the evaluator to survey or 'sample' the content any more than blocks of words.

A far more effective method is to make frequent use of sub-headings. This does enable the evaluator to see where you are going with your answer. Your material will be easier to understand if you give the reader an opportunity to pause and 'breathe'. Sub-headings help to do this; so do short paragraphs. Aim not to exceed six or seven lines as a rule. Use visual style to reinforce the structure and hierarchy of your material – for example, a larger font for main headings than for sub-headings (where permitted).

Having decided on such a scheme, apply it consistently throughout. Whether the text is laid out in columns or runs across the page, a consistently-applied left hand margin gives the page an orderly and clean appearance. Therefore it is better to avoid using indentations to distinguish between levels of sub-points.

Graphics

Images often have the capacity to get a point across with an immediacy and impact that words cannot compete with. Perhaps because the law is such a verbally-orientated profession, graphics tend to be an under-used resource in legal proposals. Authors should think about which messages and material could be best-conveyed using images. Common examples include:

The group photo: particularly where a joint bid is being made by separate firms or the team comprises staff from different countries, a good group photo underpins the message: 'these people can and do work together'.

The organogram: a spoke and hub design can be used to emphasise co-ordination and flat management structures, compared with the traditional 'family tree' lay out.

Gantt/flow charts: together with variants, these are probably the most commonly used graphics in proposals. They are ideal for showing chronological processes and the expected completion of project stages against deadlines.

Pie charts: they are mainly for getting across messages about proportionality. For example, if you wanted to show that partner time will be a substantial slice of the total number of hours to be committed to a project.

Bar/line charts: these are best for showing trends – such as the firm reaching a rising number of KPI targets over a five-year period.

Graphics should not be used just to break up the text or because they look pretty. The message they get across – and its relevance to the topic at hand – must be immediately apparent to the reader. If it is not clear how the words and graphics are working together, the visual elements may seem like a distraction or even self-indulgence. For the same reason, avoid using multiple graphics to illustrate a single topic.

Where the tender is of a reasonable size it is common practice to design a cover specifically for the bid, reflecting a theme that is relevant to the prospective client. In other professions and sectors, the organisation's logo is often reproduced in headers or footers throughout the document. Law firms can do the same (although they ought perhaps to be punctilious about getting permission to do so).

Tools and templates

We have said that content which is explicitly tailored to the prospective client's organisation will have much more impact than general 'boilerplate'. Procurement professionals often express contempt for boilerplate – making the point that it is immediately obvious when firms produce standard text that could have been written for any potential client. The failure to produce a sufficiently tailored proposal (to the organisation or to the specific requirements of the assignment) is the most common reason for firms to receive a low score or be eliminated from the competition.

This does not mean that it is not permissible to recycle material that has been used in past tenders. Anyone regularly involved in tendering will have drawn on previous proposals, a library of topic-related information or templates of various kinds. The key to avoiding the boilerplate trap is to start with a blank sheet of paper, define what the buyers are looking for (or clarify what they are asking) and only then consider how to use pre-prepared material.

Template types

It is also helpful to distinguish between different types of template. These might be referred to as standard, model and illustrative text:

Standard text
Standard text requires no alteration from one tender to the next (although it will probably need updating from time to time). This usually applies to a number of the pre-qualification questions which public sector and larger corporate organisations tend to ask. Examples include details of insurances, the firm's latest accounts, letters from the bank confirming financial standing and from the tax authority confirming that tax liabilities have been paid promptly.

Model text
Model text refers to pre-prepared material which can be used as a starting point when drafting parts of the latest tender, provided it is amended to reflect the particularities of the prospective client and the assignment. This might include policies relating to health & safety, the environment, diversity, corporate social responsibility and so on. It is a mistake to assume that the firm's standard statements in these areas will do.

Other areas where model text is appropriate are profiles of team members and description of process, for example service methodology and quality assurance. A lot of the graphics you might want to use will also fall into this category.

Illustrative text
The purpose of illustrative text is to provide examples of what authors should be aiming to achieve - without giving them something they can copy. Being highly tailored to a specific situation, the text will not be transferable from its original context to another.

This will usually apply to the most prominent sections of the document, questions with the heaviest weighting and the areas that are likely to be the most influential in determining the outcome. For example: the executive summary; key messages; the substance of the solution you are putting forward; and responses to questions that ask about your understanding of the assignment, and what your differentiators are.

The most critical point is that pre-prepared files should be accompanied by clear direction on how and when to use them. Authors need to be reminded at every opportunity to address the individual characteristics of the buyer and the bid.

Proposal automation software

Various web-based systems are available that enable multiple authors to contribute to the development of the bid, under the direction and control of a central coordinator or editor. Other systems use automation software to simplify and reduce the costs of putting together the tender. Tools currently in use include:

Library of pre-approved proposal and RFP content
A first draft can be put together quickly, making the bid team more productive while ensuring that all documents reflect consistent messages and contain only approved material. The software also expedites the review process by restricting reviewer comment to specific sections of the RFP response, and assigning and tracking due dates for input.

Access to wider content
This enables users to gain access to suitable material contained in documents developed while delivering projects for clients, rather than just pre-written content specifically developed and held for proposals.

Sales enablement tools
These are intended to reduce the time it takes to locate, personalise and deliver sales materials within the organisation. It has been suggested that business development can spend as much as 20 per cent of its time finding and validating information for credentials statements, proposals and other external communications.

Although a number of firms are employing automation software, some users believe it may entrench the habit of reaching for boilerplate when the proposal team really need to be thinking about the particular requirements of the bid. An automated system is no substitute for having authors or bid managers who know where to go in the firm for the best material and how to adapt it to the context.

Reviewing and improving the draft

You may be given a draft of the document to review, usually with limited time before the deadline, or you may wish to stand back and assess your own work. In either case, a checklist can be helpful in quickly highlighting areas of the text that need attention and can be improved.

CHECKLIST: Reviewing and Improving the Draft

Does the submission comply with what was requested?

Start with the most basic thing: get hold of the RFP and make sure that the draft complies with the instructions. As editor or reviewer, you are a key line of defence against any weaknesses in that respect. And you may be surprised how often a requirement in the RFP has been overlooked or misinterpreted.

If the document is in the form of a questionnaire response, start by reading the first paragraph of each answer. As mentioned above, it is common for authors to answer the question they would prefer to have been asked rather than the one that was actually asked. The opening paragraph needs to get across the essence of your response to that question. You cannot afford to waste space on oblique preamble.

Do we articulate why we should be chosen?

As discussed earlier in the chapter, whether or not the tender is in questionnaire format you should have an opening statement which in three or four short paragraphs gets across your firm's case for being selected. This is unlikely to be convincing unless the summary and other key sections of the document are tailored to the recipient and articulate how the organisation will gain from working with you (see below). The reasons you advance for being selected will be a combination of benefits you will bring to the client and evidence that you can deliver on those promises.

As reviewer, you will check that there is such an opening statement and that the key messages it conveys stand up to scrutiny.

Is the document specific to the client?

Put simply: could this document have been written only for this client, by only your firm? Many authors think that they are tailoring the document merely by frequently citing the client's name – but nobody's going to be fooled by that. The text needs to refer to the specific issues facing the organisation and how your firm is going to tackle those issues in delivering the service. It needs to include evidence of your ability to solve problems and add value.

Do we explain how the client will benefit?

Fee-earners are inclined to write at length about the processes they will employ in carrying out the service, without articulating how the client will gain from these activities. Apply the 'so what?' test to such narrative. As reviewer, you need to identify all the areas in the text where benefits could be expressed more effectively. However, take a tough line on any assertions which are not supported by evidence - as the evaluator will.

Does each sentence need to be read once-only?

Your aim is to ensure that text is easy to understand and quick to read. The twin peaks of good business writing therefore are clarity and economy.

A useful benchmark when reviewing the draft is to try to ensure that the evaluator will not have to read any sentence more than once in order to absorb its meaning. Any that you stumble over should be edited or queried.

Look out for common weaknesses – for example, sentences which strain the reader's concentration by being repetitious, containing redundant words or cramming in too many sub-clauses. Another case for vigilance is excessive use of the passive voice. This often creates the impression that the authors want to distance themselves from the commitments made in the document, and a sense of ambiguity about who is going to do what on the assignment.

Does the appearance of the document make it more attractive to read?

Many legal tenders make the reader feel as if they have entered a dense forest where all the trees look the same and where you are bound to lose your sense of direction. Coherent layout is as important to readability as coherent language. Consciously or unconsciously, the evaluator will be influenced by the navigability of the document as a whole and the individual sections within it. He or she should be able to see at a glance which territory is covered within a section and what the main landmarks are.

When reviewing the document, check to ensure that the headings and sub-headings conform to a consistent hierarchy, and that it is easy for the reader to distinguish between them. Where there are dense blocks of text, think how the page can be given visual relief. Break up long paragraphs and use subheadings frequently. The subheadings themselves should provide a guiding path through the narrative. Use graphics, but only if their relevance is immediately apparent to the reader.

Does the document show that we pay close attention to detail?

Rooting out spelling or grammatical mistakes is important not only for its own sake but also because it sends a message to the reader that you care about detail. Naturally, the buyers of legal services expect their advisers to be good at detail and are apt to attach symbolic significance to errors of this kind. A typical line of thought is "if they are sloppy putting together the tender document, are they going to be sloppy in delivering the service?"

A more common fault - one that is often not dealt with as thoroughly – is a failure to ensure consistency of style, for example in connection with the use of acronyms and terms of address. Your intention is to create the impression that the document has been written by a single author – otherwise you are likely to send the wrong message about the firm's ability to be cohesive.

In respect of some of the points above, you may be able to improve the document without further input from the author. However, editing in isolation seldom produces the best results and wherever possible you should engage the author on the issues you have identified in your review. The checklist should help to structure that discussion and expedite progress in producing a better draft.

Roles in producing the submission

Bid managers have a key role to play in helping to prepare the document: this is one of the areas where they can provide the most practical benefits to the service team. Their involvement may include:

- Taking on much of the burden of drafting and producing the document, freeing the proposed service team to concentrate on preparing for and engaging in direct contact with the decision-makers;

- Helping the team to develop and refine key messages, including challenging ideas which have not been fully thought through and claims which are not supported with evidence;

- Ensuring that the visual style of the document is attractive and enhances or reinforces the content; and

- Ensuring that the team is aware of and complies with drafting, review and production deadlines.

At the same time, partners and senior fee earners are likely to be closest to the decision-makers and have the best understanding of the organisation's objectives and requirements. Without getting bogged down in producing text, partners need to provide a thorough briefing to authors if the latter are to produce quality material.

eProcurement

Although eProcurement embraces the whole tender process, it fundamentally affects the transmission and receipt of tender documentation and can therefore be considered under the heading of the written submission. It has become a well-established feature of the bidding landscape, particularly where the contracting organisations are large or the contract value is substantial. eProcurement encompasses three sub-disciplines: eTendering, eEvaluation and eAuctions.

eTendering

eTendering uses web-based technology to enable buyers and suppliers to manage their interactions securely online during the tender process. The tools support the full tender process including advertisement, expression of interest, pre-qualification, invitation to tender and award notices.

In the public sector it can be used for procurements of any category, size, complexity and value. The procuring authority sets up a secure website (often referred to in the public notice) on which it publishes a notice, inviting bidders to respond using a web-form. The software can select qualifying bidders and provide non-qualifiers with the reasons why they have been excluded. However, a human element is always incorporated into the process through a review of the results and in investigating any challenges from non-qualifiers. As well as web-forms, eTendering can accept proposal documents in the form of attachments.

In the private sector, eTendering platforms often form part of wider spend and contract management systems. One example widely used across industry is Ariba. Sector-specific platforms have also been launched.

eEvaluation

eEvaluation refers to web-based technology that enables client teams, often located in different parts of the country, to work collaboratively. It allows them to develop evaluation plans, structure assessment criteria, evaluate tender documentation and carry out bid comparisons in a secure, common working environment. eEvaluation is most suitable for strategic procurements or where qualitative evaluation is needed, and can be used in conjunction with eTendering.

When involved in a tender using eEvaluation, it is essential to follow all instructions to the letter. It may not be apparent why particular formats or naming protocols have been stipulated – but often there are specific technical reasons for the instructions.

Find out how the document is being evaluated. In particular, ensure you understand the protocols governing the division of responsibilities amongst evaluators. Will they get to read the whole document, or will the remit of the evaluation team be split? This may influence the way you approach the tender submission.

Bid evaluation software is not designed to assess the quality of proposals, other than in pure compliance terms. The software assists with the logistics of the tender without any artificial intelligence element. However, it may have encouraged some clients to use the word-search facility (something in fact they could equally do with most non-specialist applications if a proposal has been submitted electronically) to draw some conclusions about the bid. Even where separate teams are assigned to evaluating different parts of the response, bidders must take care to avoid contradictions or inconsistencies across the tender, as these may be easily highlighted if an evaluator chooses to search for a key word or phrase such as 'litigation risk' or 'quality control'.

Evaluators may also search for words or phrases which they feel could compromise the bidders' proposals in some way. Therefore bidders need to exercise care in using qualifying language such as 'but', 'however' 'notwithstanding', 'in development' and so on. Remember that your evaluators are more likely to search for their own organisation's jargon than your firm's.

eAuctions

An eAuction is a web-based framework for conducting real time negotiations in which the buyer invites pre-approved suppliers to participate in simultaneous online negotiation in placing their best and final bids. The process should follow strict rules and be conducted in a completely secure and transparent manner.

Three methods are used in conducting eAuctions. Using the phased method, participants are required to submit a bid when directed by the 'auctioneer'. With the fixed time method, bidders are given a designated period (usually half an hour) in which to make their bid. The fixed time-with-extension method is designed to overcome the distortions of participants putting in a bid at the last minute - which is what tends to happen with the fixed time option.

In deciding whether an eAuction is appropriate, public sector purchasers are advised to take account of market factors such as the level of competition and similarity or otherwise of suppliers and their capabilities and offerings. In some countries contracting authorities are advised that eAuctions should follow a non-price based evaluation rather than be stand-alone.

In the private sector, eAuctions are high profile and said to be increasing in frequency. There is a school of thought that eAuctions encourage bidders to bid at an unsustainable level – so the method is considered to be controversial. However, research (by Huthwaite International) suggests that reverse auctions have been used to persuade suppliers to bid lower than they need to. While the auctioneers often imply that the contract will be automatically awarded to the lowest bidder, this is not necessarily the case.

New formats

Across industry, new technologies are having an impact on the bidding process. For example, 3-D printing has provided architects and construction companies with a cheap method of creating structural models. A new technology used by law firms in the bidding arena is the app.

An app provides options for presenting material which are beyond the reach of conventional documents. Project timelines and credentials such as global coverage can often be conveyed more effectively using dynamic rather than static graphics. Video clips can bring CVs to life and add a documentary quality to case studies.

Apps may also help to inform the approach to the rest of the bid: embedded analytics can show which team members are attracting the most interest – and therefore give a steer on who to include in the presentation, or who should have the most prominent roles on the engagement.

It is not just their technical capacities which might encourage more firms to look at using them in bids. For the moment, there's likely to be novelty value in doing so; an option to be considered whenever the prospective client is adjudged to be susceptible to the Wow factor.

Ironically perhaps for a high tech solution, the preferred means of getting the app into the decision-makers' hands is often distinctly traditional – a courier delivers a tablet containing the app to each recipient. This reflects the more stringent requirements for confidentiality and security associated with proposals. It helps to ensure the content is seen only by those for whom it is intended; if a tablet goes astray, it can be locked remotely. Given tighter ant-bribery regulations in a number of jurisdictions, it is prudent to inform recipients that the tablets are not gifts and will be collected on a pre-arranged date.

What other constraints should firms take into account? You cannot use an app to surprise and impress a prospective client when the delivery format has been specified in advance. Some would not be impressed anyway. The cost of developing the app needs to be taken into consideration. That will depend on functionality and the number of pages to be coded, but it is likely to be significantly more expensive than the hard copy version – however glossy.

The time required to develop and test the app can add to deadline pressure, although the first time will be the most time consuming – the timetable can be cut 40 to 60 per cent for subsequent versions.

Perhaps most important, remember that the medium is not a substitute for the message. In the words of one business development director who has been through the process: "do not let the delivery mechanism drive the strategy. You have to guard against being seduced by what the app can do, when that might obscure the critical messages you're trying to get across".

Chapter 6 at a glance:
The Submission

Context

Bidders need to be aware of the context in which the tender response has been requested. In many type 1 tenders, the submission is principally a means of gathering information and is a preliminary step towards selecting the winning firm. In many type 2 tenders, by contrast, the evaluation of the written submission determines the outcome.

The free-form proposal

Where the structure of the document is left to the bidders' discretion, the authors should ensure that material likely to have the most impact on the reader is given a prominent position. This includes how the firm proposes to tackle the assignment, drawing on ISBE principles as described in chapter 5; and details on the key members of the team.

The summary should be kept to one page and articulate why the buyers should choose you. Keep it to no more than three or four points. In each point say how the prospective client will benefit from your involvement and highlight evidence that shows you can deliver.

Questionnaires

Particularly for questions that carry a heavy weighting in the evaluation, you need to summarise the key points of your answer in the first paragraph. Avoid preamble and make sure that the response is strictly relevant. Leave out value judgements about the firm's attributes and statements that cannot be independently verified.

To achieve the highest scores, you need to show how you will apply your expertise in the context of the client's specific objectives and circumstances; and describe the benefits you can provide that go beyond the formal requirements of the contract.

Visual style

Even with the type of document that offers little scope for visual presentation, the layout of the page is important. It needs to convey a sense of order and to enable the reader to see at a glance the ground you are covering in a section or answer.

Layout, visual devices and graphics should reinforce the key messages you are trying to convey. The meaning of a table or visual must be instantly comprehensible to the reader.

Tools and templates

While material used for previous proposals can play a helpful role in putting together the tender response, on substantive questions or sections evaluators will be unimpressed with anything that that reads like boilerplate.

Templates however can speed up the preparation process. It is important to distinguish between sections where exactly the same material can be recycled (such as in responses to purely factual pre-qualification questions) and those where previous answers are just a starting point for producing material which needs to be precisely tailored to the exercise at hand. With the most critical sections, such as the summary, it is best to start with a blank sheet of paper.

Reviewing and improving the draft

Work through a checklist of key questions to identify quickly areas where the submission can be improved. Does it comply with what was requested? Do we articulate why we should be chosen? Is the document specific to the client? Do we explain how the client will benefit? Is the meaning of each sentence clear without having to re-read it? Does the appearance of the document make it more attractive to read? Does it show we play close attention to detail?

Roles in producing the submission

Bid managers have a key role to play in helping to prepare the document. At the same time, partners and senior fee-earners are likely to have the best understanding of the organisation's objectives and requirements. Without getting bogged down in producing text, partners need to provide a thorough briefing if the bid team is to produce quality material.

eProcurement

The use of on-line portals to administer the tender process (eTendering) is common practice in both the private and public sector. eEvaluation – web-based technology that allows evaluators in physically remote locations to collaborate with each other – has been used in connection with legal services. Evaluators can use word search facilities to identify phrases that they feel might compromise bidders' proposals.

eAuctions are generally associated with the procurement of commodity goods and services but have also been used in the selection of professional advisers, including law firms.

New formats

Some law firms have used computer apps as a format for the tender submission – particularly for clients in digital-related industries. Apps provide options for presenting material that are beyond the reach of conventional documents. This includes dynamic graphics and video clips to bring team profiles and case studies to life. Ultimately, however, the proposal will only be as good as its content – however slick the presentation.

7. The Presentation

Context
Your objectives
Reconnaissance
Selecting the presenters
Structure and content
Delivery
Team cohesion
Preparation and rehearsal
Follow-up

Context

The shift from the type 1 to type 2 proposal model means that presentations play a less influential role in many tenders than they once did. In public sector bids often the presentation does not contribute to the evaluation, or there is no requirement for one at all. This practice is being increasingly adopted by corporate and institutional buyers.

The shift in emphasis away from oral communication in the proposal process reflects the procurement department's agenda of wanting to 'objectify' decision-making. Panel members' reaction to and assessment of the presentation is regarded as being more subjective than an evaluator's analysis of a written response. The latter leaves an audit trail that can be examined later if required; a presentation (unless recorded) is lost in the moment of delivery.

In spite of this, there are still a great many legal tenders where a presentation is required. Where that is the case, it is likely to have a much greater influence on the outcome than anything else.

There is no doubt that face-to-face encounters, whether at the presentation or earlier on in the process, have an impact on decision-makers which the written word does not. As discussed in the previous chapter, anyone who regularly conducts proposal debriefs knows that decision-makers are likely to have a much more vivid recollection of the oral than the written part of the exercise. Instinctively, they will often answer a question about the document by referring to what one of the presenters said at the meeting. In many cases, a team's performance at the presentation is the decisive factor in awarding the contract.

It follows that in those tenders where the presentation is likely to be influential in determining the outcome, this part of the process should warrant the most attention and energy from the senior members of the team. In practice this is seldom the case. There may be cultural reasons for that. In carrying out their work, lawyers are required to pay close attention to the written word; oral communication is perhaps considered to be less important.

Often that attitude is reflected in the approach to tenders. Many corporate lawyers are self-confident communicators, comfortable with extemporising in public, and do not feel they need to prepare for or rehearse a presentation very thoroughly.

This is a mistake. As we shall see, some of the factors that will make a presentation effective and persuasive have nothing to do with an individual presenter's accomplishments as a public speaker.

Your objectives

In a seminar or speech, your primary purpose might be to impart information or rally support for a cause. In a pitch, your objective is to create a picture of what you will be like to work with.

To have reached this stage, the decision-makers will usually have already concluded that your firm has the technical capabilities to do the job. In the presentation the emphasis should hence not be on rehearsing your credentials. What they are interested in is how the relationship will work in practice. That is likely to include making an assessment of: how adept you will be at putting legal problems in a commercial context; your understanding of the issues from the legal department's point of view; and how supportive you will be to this team and to operational management.

The panel will be sitting through a number of presentations covering similar ground, often taking place back-to-back or within a short period. The question then is how to stand out from the rest.

The new business pitch is not just another exercise in public speaking: it has specific dynamics and objectives which need to be reflected in how you prepare for it.

Reconnaissance

The first objective is to ensure your pitch is appropriate to the circumstances in which it is taking place and the requirements of the audience. You should therefore find out as much as you can about the arrangements for the presentation and the decision-makers' expectations of it. That could include the following:

CHECKLIST: Presentation Due Diligence

General reactions to the written proposal (where one has been submitted in advance of the meeting); areas covered that might be expanded on in the presentation; other issues to focus on

Who/how many we should include in the presentation team (taking account of the above where applicable)

Who/how many will attend from their side

Overall duration of the meeting and expected split between the formal presentation and Q&A

The features and dimensions of the room where you will be presenting

Where you will be asked to sit/stand in relation to the panel

Whether or not you are expected to use visual aids and details of facilities, e.g. flip charts, projector or screen

Your contact at the organisation may be non-committal on many of these points, but it can only help to clarify the decision-makers' preferences where they exist. A member of the presentation team should visit the venue in advance wherever possible.

Selecting the presenters

Without any explicit indication to the contrary, it is usually safe to assume that the panel will wish to see the people who will be most closely involved in delivering the service. In a standard tender process you will already have been asked to provide details on these individuals at the document stage. In this respect you will want to maintain continuity wherever possible. You may, however, need to take into account certain factors that might influence (or interfere with) your decision as to whom should attend.

Beware figureheads

One of these might be described as 'senior partner syndrome'. This occurs most often on opportunities perceived to be prestigious or of high value. One of the firm's most eminent members, having not been previously involved in the tender, proposes (or decides) to attend. This is often justified on the basis that the presence of someone very senior will demonstrate the firm's commitment to the prospective client.

Unless handled carefully, such an intervention can have negative effects (also cited in chapter 1):

> "A very senior partner turned up, but he hadn't been involved before the presentation and did not understand the detail of what we wanted. We assumed he would be just a figurehead, and of no value to us."

Overwhelmingly, clients say they want WYSIWYG (What You See Is What You Get) from their advisers - starting with the tender and continuing throughout the relationship. They are likely to be suspicious of individuals they meet whom they think will either will not have an active role on the engagement or be replaced by someone more junior once the contract has been secured.

If a senior partner insists on attending a presentation in the above circumstances, it is all the more important to describe precisely what his or her role is going to be on the assignment; or, if that does not apply, why they are present. For example, it may be appropriate to get this individual to talk about the firm's wider resources and to confirm that the team leader will have the authority to draw on these as necessary. Above all, they should not usurp the team leader's role in chairing and orchestrating the presentation.

Balance between partners and non-partners

You may need to decide whether the presentation should be attended only by partners or whether a mix between partners and more junior staff, such as associates, ought to be considered. That will depend on the circumstances, but it is wise to keep the WYSIWYG principle in mind – the people the panel want to see are the ones who will be doing a lot of the actual work. On this basis it is usually right to include at least one person who is below partner level.

How many should attend?

Particularly with tenders covering a number of legal disciplines, it is tempting to include a wide range of specialists in the presentation. The relevant expert will then be on hand to explain your approach and deal with questions.

Team leaders however should be aware that their job will get harder as the size of the team grows. This is because they need to create an impression of a closely-knit group working in unity to achieve the client's goals (see 'Creating team cohesion' below). Their ability to do so will tend to be compromised by having a large number present. It is also likely to make the formal part of the presentation longer.

Absentees

It sometimes happens that a member of the team that you had intended to include in the presentation cannot attend – perhaps because of an existing client commitment. Generally, prospective clients will be understanding about this. It will do you no harm to get across the message that you will not put the prospect of new business ahead of looking after existing clients – something they may find reassuring if they are to become one.

You might suggest that the individual in question is replaced on the day with a close colleague (incidentally showing that the firm has strength in depth in the relevant discipline). It may also be possible to arrange for the absentee to meet with the panel on another occasion.

As with so may other aspects of the tender process, maintaining dialogue with the decision-makers and ascertaining what their preferences are will put you at an advantage.

Structure and content

Unless directed otherwise, the formal part of the presentation should comprise three elements: an introduction, the main body, and the summing up. The lead partner should be responsible for doing the introduction and summing up, and may also have a substantive topic to cover as well. In that case, it should usually be slotted in immediately before the summing up. To keep the presentation within a streamlined, economical framework, the lead partner should have not more than two speaking slots; other members of the team should have one only.

Duration

Usually you will be given an indication of how long your meeting is scheduled for (an hour is typical), though not always how the time should divide between the formal part of the presentation and the Q&A. In the absence of any clear indication, 25 minutes for the formal part is long enough – after that the panel will tend to lose concentration.

The opening

These sessions often begin with the lead partner making some cordial remarks, such as thanking the panel for inviting the firm to present. Many find a way of dragging this out for a minute or two, perhaps feeling they need to warm up the audience before getting on to anything interesting. Then they introduce their colleagues around the table, in a similarly low-key fashion.

Such an opening is hardly likely to set the world on fire – and it is a wasted opportunity. The beginning of the presentation is perhaps the only time when you can be certain that you have the panel's undivided attention.

Far better to start with a hard-hitting scene-setter: an overview of what the firm sees as the challenges facing the company and the role legal advisers can play in overcoming them. The subject matter will vary. But the essential point is to create an impression from the outset that you are outward-looking, interested in the prospective client's business and capable of grasping the commercial implications of the advice you will be giving.

This is a far more dynamic way of opening the presentation. But it needs to be kept short: Anything longer than a minute and the panel will be wondering when the other members of the team are going to get in on the act.

Having provided an appetiser of what is to follow, the lead partner should then introduce his or her colleagues – do not leave them to introduce themselves (see 'Team cohesion' below). These team introductions need to be approached systematically and require careful preparation. For each individual, they should comprise three elements:

- The role he or she will play on the assignment
- Why this individual is particularly well qualified to fulfil the role, with reference to relevant client experience
- The areas he or she will cover during the presentation

Only a sentence or two may be required for each, although the lead partner may wish to elaborate a little further on the individual's experience and achievements where these are of particular interest or relevance.

Tender responses in the legal sector often say too little about who will be doing what on a day-to-day basis – whether a matter or task will be handled by a partner or an assistant. In any event, the introductions provide an opportunity to clarify the roles that the team will play. This approach also enables the lead partner to create a strong platform for the other speakers and to signpost the overall structure of the presentation. After talking about their colleagues, lead partners should introduce themselves in the same way.

The panel will find it easier to absorb this information if it is presented in the same order for each member of the team.

The main body

This is the part where team members other than the lead partner get to speak. Usually each presenter will cover a distinct aspect of the organisation's requirements. In many cases the material will be based on the value propositions put forward in the document – you will wish to focus on issues which you believe are likely to be of particular importance to the panel, perhaps exploring a new angle or looking at the topic in greater depth.

As with the value propositions developed in the written submission, the ISBE framework is a good starting point (see chapter 5). Explain why the issue is important; propose a solution (or outline possible options that might lead there); articulate and if possible quantify the benefits that will result; and provide evidence to support your claims. It is even more important to use practical examples and illustrations at the presentation: the points you make will be the more memorable when put into a practical context.

Only talk about your own or the firm's achievements and experience in the context of the issues facing the prospective client and the benefits you expect to generate through your approach and involvement. Remember, by the presentation stage the evaluators are likely to have already satisfied themselves that you are technically capable of doing the work. To spend precious time reiterating your credentials is to miss the point of the occasion.

Bear in mind 'the power of three' – most people find it easy to remember three items but will often forget something if there are more than that. When a speaker wants to make six points, the audience will find them more memorable if they are presented as two groups of three.

The summing up

As with the executive summary or covering letter in the written submission, the purpose of the summing up is not to summarise all the material that has been presented, but to articulate the reasons why your firm should be chosen. You may wish to use the summary in the document as a template. For the presentation, a shortened and simplified version is likely to be required.

However, the same principles apply. Nobody is going to remember ten reasons why you should be selected: leave them with no more than three or four key messages. These should comprise a concise phrase or sentence – a 'sound bite' short enough to lodge in the minds of the decision-makers – supported by a few sentences which incorporate the most persuasive evidence at your disposal. The lead partner should also use the summing up to refer back the contributions from the other members of the team (see 'Team cohesion' below).

Delivery

Consciously or unconsciously, the decision-makers will draw inferences from your presentation about how the relationship will work in practice – your ability to grasp the issues which are important to the client, to show an appreciation of the risks and opportunities from the organisation's perspective, to give a clear recommendation on the best way forward and so on.

To some extent, you want the presentation to resemble the sort of meeting you might have with the client once you are working on the assignment. The tone should be conversational but business-like. At the same time you need to build in an element of "theatre" as well, in order to gain and keep the panel's attention.

Be wary of devices or tools which could act as a barrier between you and the decision-makers, or anything which obstructs their ability to form an impression of what you are going to be like to work with in practice. Think of slides and scripts – would you use these in a normal business meeting? They can undermine your efforts to build rapport. These points are discussed in more detail below.

Signposting

For the panel members, your presentation is unfamiliar terrain – they need some landmarks and signposts to help them navigate their way through it. The signposts may or may not be visual (see 'Using visual aids' below), but they should be built into the presenter's speech. Tell your audience what you are going to say, say it, then tell them what you have said.

Provide a brief overview of the ground you intend to cover and enumerate the points as you proceed to help orientate panel members and enable them to keep track of the structure. Audiences which lose sight of this are apt to become restless and distracted – and to stop listening.

Punctuation

Oral 'punctuation' is a critical aspect of good delivery. This refers to the variations in timing, intonation and emphasis that help the speaker to arrest the panel members' attention, impress upon them the key points, give them the opportunity to digest the argument and keep them interested.

Punctuation can also be effective in building anticipation and adding an element of theatre.

Examples include using pauses to signify the transition to a new theme or applying extra emphasis to the 'sound bites' that summarise the reasons why the firm should be selected.

Using notes

It is better for the team to use notes rather than a verbatim script for the presentation, for the reason already given. Scripts introduce an element of artificiality, and formality, which do not help the presentation team to build rapport with the decision-makers or to illustrate what the working relationship will be like. Using notes rather than a script means that presenters' delivery may falter from time to time. They may not be word perfect. On the other hand – and more important – their delivery is likely to seem more natural and spontaneous.

However, the lead partner's role at the presentation goes beyond that of the other members of the team and this has a bearing on the approach he or she should take. Scene-setting and team introductions at the beginning of the presentation, and key messages at the end, require well chosen words crafted in advance. The level of precision needed will not be achieved if the lead partner relies on improvisation at these moments. He or she therefore should try to commit at least some of the key phrases to memory, and have a written version to hand as a back up.

Using visual aids

It can be a good idea to incorporate a visual dimension into the presentation. However, the way visual aids are usually applied in practice does more harm than good. Corporate lawyers tend to overuse PowerPoint. Slides work best when supporting specific points rather than providing a continuous accompaniment. The fewer that are used, the more impact they are likely to have.

The pitfalls
There are two main problems with the way PowerPoint is often used. The first lies in the idea of the slideshow itself. After the lights are dimmed, the screen becomes the main character in the drama. Research has shown that when people are simultaneously subjected to visual and aural stimulus, their attention is drawn to the visual. So the images on the screen become the

focal point of the presentation, not what the presenters are saying. This does not help the presenters convey their personalities, show what they are going to be like to work with or build rapport with the decision-makers.

The second problem is the tendency to put large amounts of written material on the slides. Presenters do this partly because they find it comforting to have a prop available. If they forget what they are supposed to be saying, they will be able to pick up the thread by looking at the screen. They may also have read somewhere that people are more likely to remember a message if they see it and hear it.

The result, however, is always unsatisfactory. If there is a conflict between the material on the screen and what the presenter is saying, the visual will simply blot out the aural: no-one can read one thing and listen to another at the same time, and properly absorb both sets of information.

If on the other hand the presenter speaks the same words that are on the slide, the effect is even worse. How can the presenter gain and hold the panel's attention if the material is already on the screen for them to read? The speaker is reduced to being a redundant voice-over.

Orientation and reinforcement
So are visual aids not appropriate for legal pitches? It depends on the circumstances. It is true that messages delivered visually and aurally can reinforce each other. In one study, participants were given some written material. They remembered 20 per cent when provided with words alone, but 40 per cent when visuals were added. Moreover, research shows that the way people respond to external stimuli varies considerably from individual to individual.

According to these sources over 30 per cent of the population as a whole respond primarily to graphical or visual stimuli, while roughly the same proportion are kinaesthetically orientated (touch and feel). Less than 30 per cent find it easiest to apprehend and interpret information conveyed through the written or spoken word. Yet the vast majority of business communication is channelled through this single medium.

Using words and images together
A presentation which uses visual as well auditory media should engage a wider audience than if one medium were used alone. The question is how to avoid the conflict (or repetition) between voice and screen that is a common feature of so many poor presentations.

The essential point is that visual imagery needs to complement and not reproduce the spoken word. That means that in most circumstances only two types of material should be put on slides: headings and graphics.

Whole sentences or even phrases that appear on the screen are likely to detract from the presenter. But headings can help the more visually orientated members of the panel absorb the overall structure of the presentation. It can help them keep abreast of the structure as it unfolds and recall key messages when the presentation is over. Key words will have greater impact if presented imaginatively, rather than in the usual bullet point template.

Graphics are best used to provide evidence to support what the presenter is saying. The most common mistake is to make them over-elaborate - time spent puzzling over the meaning of a graph is time spent not listening to the presenter. Examples of material which is often best represented graphically includes:

Team chart/linkages between the external and internal team

Statistics (e.g. as pie or bar charts)

Transaction processes (e.g. as flow charts)

Geographical coverage (e.g. using maps)

Even if applied in a disciplined way, the danger with slides is that the images rather than the presenters will become the focal point of the panel's attention. Their use needs to be carefully choreographed.

This means actively drawing the panel members' attention to the graphic, pausing to allow them to grasp its significance and highlighting or elucidating a particular aspect of it where appropriate. Then, and equally important, moving their attention away from the slide and on to the next topic.

Where the size of the contract justifies it, you may wish to consider incorporating a video sequence into PowerPoint. This can have a powerful effect – although ruthless editing is needed to ensure that this device does not become mere self-indulgence. (The same point applies to the use of visual material.) A video sequence should be introduced with an appropriate note of anticipation and at the end rounded off in such a way that the presenter can move smoothly to the next topic.

Other options
The projector or laptop screen are not the only options. Hand-outs have the advantage of being kinaesthetic as well as visual. Fine detail (such as a map or chart) will be much easier to read in a hand-out than on a slide.

On the other hand, from the presenter's point of view they can be difficult to control. Apart from sometimes being cumbersome to distribute, the presenter may find it harder to direct the audience's attention away from the hand-out when it is time to move on to the next topic. Hand out one page at a time – if not, panel members' attention will stray to the other sheets and they will stop listening to what you are saying.

Team cohesion

> "I visited a number of firms we then used as part of a review we were carrying out. At one firm it emerged the lead partner did not know what one of the other solicitors present had done for us. That was reason enough in my book to take them off the list." (Head of legal, financial institution)

One of the most consistent messages to emerge from proposal debriefs is that the ability to come across as a unified team is highly influential in determining the outcome of tenders – and on occasion is the decisive factor. Perhaps because of the collegiate roots of the profession, partners often assume they are conveying the impression of being a closely-knit group, particularly if they are used to working together. However, that is not always how things appear from the other side of the desk. In practice, careful preparation is needed to make the presenters into a seamless unit.

Critical factors

A multiplicity of factors may contribute to creating an impression of cohesion, or the lack of it. There are three areas in particular which, if not handled effectively, will tend to make decision-makers apprehensive.

Role definition
They will want to be given a concrete idea of how each person present is going to contribute to the engagement. This is often not fully addressed. A

common concern is whether a senior partner will be genuinely committed to and involved in the assignment, or will turn out to be more of a figurehead (see 'Selecting the presenters' above). Lack of clarity over such matters can create enough doubt in decision-makers' minds to put them off you.

Balance
Over-dominance by one individual can fatally undermine the presentation. What often happens is that a senior member of the team 'squeezes out' a more junior one. This deprives the panel of the opportunity to form a proper impression of the individual – someone whom they may be dealing with regularly on the assignment. Decision-makers are often reluctant to appoint a firm if they have not gained a sense of the personality and style of each of the presenters.

Mutual support
Decision-makers will certainly notice if presenters fail to support each other. This will seldom be a case of one speaker flatly contradicting another. It is more likely to take the form of team members not appearing to be fully engaged when a colleague is speaking; or seeming unsure of the ground their colleagues are intending to cover; or feeling obliged to 'rescue' another team member if they felt the response to a question was inadequate. It is quite easy to undermine a colleague without meaning to. In the somewhat artificial atmosphere of a presentation, decision-makers will be sensitive to these nuances and will be influenced by them.

Methods of reinforcing cohesion

Much of the responsibility for creating a sense of team cohesion lies with the lead partner. One of his or her main goals should be to orchestrate the presentation to achieve precisely that. The following points provide a reliable guide to good practice:

CHECKLIST: Methods of Reinforcing Cohesion

Formally introduce the other members of the team

It is usual for lead partners to make the introductions but so often the opportunity to create a sense of cohesion is missed. By explaining why each presenter has been chosen for the assignment, what their roles will be and the topics they are going to cover in the presentation, the lead partner will help to reinforce the message that this is a handpicked team – not just pairs of hands who happened to be available when the tender arrived. Showing ready familiarity with other team members' experience implies that the team leader knows what they can do and trusts them to do it well.

Create a strong platform for the other speakers

It is more convincing if the lead partner highlights the credentials and experience of the other presenters, and its relevance to the matter at hand, than if they are left to blow their own trumpets. The seniority of the lead partner means that his or her endorsement will carry authority. This narrative also provides a subliminal confirmation that the lead partner has a detailed grasp of their professional achievements and ability to add value.

Ensure roles are clearly defined

Job titles are not enough. Decision-makers often want to know how much time the key members of the team will devote to the assignment and how that time will be spent; how the individuals' expertise will fit together and how their level of seniority and experience will be matched to the tasks to be undertaken.

Orchestrate the transitions between speakers

One simple illustration of the need to prepare carefully for presentations is that, without the benefit of a rehearsal, the hand-overs between speakers almost always sound clumsy and tentative. Speakers should have a strong cadence with which to finish their part of the presentation, but then need do no more than look at the team leader who will ask the next speaker to begin. This highlights another factor which is important in creating the impression of a tightly-knit team: eye contact.

Use eye contact

Everybody understands that eye contact is essential in engaging an audience, especially in the relatively intimate environment of the presentation where people will usually be gathered around a boardroom table. What is often overlooked, however, is that eye contact is equally important between members of the team. Decision-makers will want to feel that the speakers are aware of, and listening to, what each other are saying. Active engagement between team members is essential if that is to come across.

Build in cross-references between presenters

Another way to demonstrate that team members are in tune with each other is for presenters to refer to other parts of the presentation and to what their colleagues have said or are going to say. Team members need to show they are thinking about each other's roles and the team's overall message, not just their contribution to it.

Ensure that everyone present has an active role

Nothing is more likely to make decision-makers uncomfortable than if one of the presentation team does not contribute. In their minds, no role on the presentation will suggest no role on the assignment. This is true both for the formal part of the presentation and the Q&A.

Aim for individual presentations to be of roughly the same length

As already discussed, it is apparent from debriefs that over-dominance by one individual (often the team leader) creates a negative impression and that presentation teams should aim to achieve a roughly equal balance between contributions.

Refer back to team members in the summing up

In summing up, the team leader should take the opportunity to underline the integrated character of the presentation, and of the team, by referring back to some of the points made by the other speakers.

Co-ordinate responses to questions

The team leader should orchestrate and co-ordinate the responses – deciding as a far as possible who will deal with each question, and inviting other members of the team to provide supplementary comments where appropriate. By actively chairing the Q&A in this way, the leader can help to ensure that all members of the team have a chance to make their mark.

You may decide not to apply every one of these instructions in every situation, but it is worth keeping them in mind to ensure nothing obvious is overlooked. Getting across the idea that the team is a genuine unit – and therefore capable of acting as a cohesive force on behalf of the client – may be one of the less tangible factors influencing the outcome of tenders. But there is no doubt it is one of the most important.

Preparation and rehearsal

Appointing a moderator

Ideally, preparation and rehearsal should be under the guidance of someone outside the proposed service team. This might be the business development director, a specialist consultant or a partner acting in a counselling role, or a combination of these. Part of their role will be to provide objective input as the presentation team members develop and try out their material. They may also be responsible for organising the mock panel and identifying questions that the panel might ask (see below).

Collective preparation

In light of everything that has been said about cohesion and co-ordination, it is impossible to overestimate the importance of the team getting together to discuss and rehearse the presentation. While rehearsals provide an opportunity for individual participants to polish their delivery, the main purpose is to get the team dynamics right and to address the points discussed in the section above.

The amount of time that should be set aside for rehearsing will depend on the circumstances. In addition to that required for presenters to develop and practise their material on their own, the team should also prepare collectively on at least three separate occasions. It is likely that the team will need to run through its presentation more than once at each rehearsal.

Initial meeting: Discuss the overall structure and main themes of the presentation; identify biographical details to be incorporated into the lead partner's opening; agree who will cover which topics; outline issues, solutions, benefits and evidence; articulate and challenge the firm's case for being selected; consider questions that the panel may ask and how the team should respond.

First rehearsal: Live run-through followed by review of structure (including timings), content, delivery and team dynamics. First Q&A role play; discuss how responses can be improved.

Second rehearsal: Taking place preferably at least 24 hours after the first rehearsal, and at least 24 hours before the presentation itself. Live run-through and second Q&A role play. Agree on and incorporate final adjustments.

The mock panel

It is common practice for presentation teams in the legal sector to be put through their paces by a group of their peers who role-play the panel. However, too often this exercise is interpreted by mock panellists as an invitation to deploy the full range of their forensic skills to deconstruct and dismantle everything the presentation team says. For lawyers, that is natural - but not necessarily helpful.

Of course the presenters need to listen to feedback, and make adjustments accordingly. If not managed properly, however, criticism of this sort can germinate creeping doubts in the presenters' minds, precisely at the moment when they most need to have confidence in their material.

The larger the panel at the dry run, the greater the tendency for presenters to be given conflicting advice. This is inevitable, as the mock panellist's reactions to what the presenters are saying, and how they are saying it, is bound to differ. But mixed messages create uncertainty and will be particularly unwelcome from the presenter's point of view if the presentation is imminent.

Colleagues sometimes have their own preconceptions about the issues being discussed and this may be reflected in the questions they put to the team. Everyone present, however, should have a shared understanding of what the strategy is for winning the work. Otherwise at least some of the comments and suggestions are likely to be confusing, or simply irrelevant.

In spite of these caveats, mock panels can have a useful function as long as their input is carefully orchestrated in advance. If acting as moderator, think about the following:

Timing
Timing can be critical. There is a tendency for presenters to put their colleagues off until the final rehearsal, because they do not feel ready before then. It is better though to hold the mock panel session at a relatively early stage. Then the presenters will have enough time to take in the feedback and become thoroughly familiar with any changes which need to be incorporated. One possibility is to invite the panel for a second run-through at the first rehearsal.

Briefing
Above all, brief the mock panel in advance about: the decision-makers; the team's strategy for winning the proposal; how it intends to deal with particular issues; competitive strengths and weaknesses; and what the key messages are. Mock panellists should also be given some guidance on how to assess the presenters (see below).

Assigning roles
Restrict the number of people attending the dry run and assign each a distinctive role: so much the better if members of the mock panel can 'shadow' specific decision-makers who will be at the presentation. It is also a good idea to have one or two people present who are not required to role play the decision-makers and ask questions, but are there purely as observers.

The Q&A

Decision-makers often say that the Q&A is likely to have more bearing on the outcome than the formal part of the presentation, or any other part of the tender process. In practice it tends not to get the rehearsal time it deserves. The moderator can play a useful role in:

Anticipating questions
In addition to inviting the presenters to identify questions they are likely to be asked (and which they would find difficult to answer), the moderator should independently compile a list of potential questions. He or she may wish to consult colleagues familiar with the relevant areas of work, the sector or the organisation itself. The moderator should also be able to draw on a bank of standard questions, based on what selection panels have asked presentation teams in previous tenders (see chapter 2).

In addition to points relating to the specific tender, the following are among the most commonly asked questions at presentations:

CHECKLIST: Questions Frequently Asked at Presentations

Capacity and continuity

How much time do the key members of the team expect to spend on the assignment?

How will you ensure that we are treated as a priority, given your other commitments?

How do you ensure continuity of service in the event of an unforeseen absence of a team member? What is your track record in this respect?

Contract management

How do you propose to monitor and report progress on outstanding matters, and which reporting formats and methods would you recommend?

How would you propose that we measure your performance?

Which KPIs do your other clients use to measure your performance? Which might be appropriate on this contract?

Fees and value for money

Your fee rates are higher than some of the other firms involved in the tender. Is there scope for us to agree to lower rates?

Would you be willing to consider alternative fee arrangements, such as performance related fees? How would this work in practice?

On other contracts, how accurate have you been in estimating costs?

Differentiation

What makes you firm different from your competitors?

Why should we appoint your firm to the contract?

What additional value would we gain from employing your firm?

Rehearsing answers

In addition to helping the team to think through how best to respond, the moderator needs to ensure the Q&A is managed effectively. He or she needs to make sure:

- The lead partner actively chairs the session. This includes co-ordinating the presenters' responses and giving everyone there an opportunity to contribute;

- Responses are concise. Long, meandering answers tend to sound defensive. They will also send the wrong message about the team's ability to give clear advice and recommendations.

Finishing on a high note

Studies have shown that it is the beginning and end of any performance that audiences are most likely to remember. The lead partner should therefore prepare a very brief statement to round off the presentation. This might echo the scene-setter at the start, while incorporating any particularly significant points raised in the Q&A. This is also an opportunity to reiterate the firm's enthusiasm to work with the prospective client.

The lead partner should also prepare a suitable response in the event that the chairman of the panel asks the presenters if they have any questions. In this case, do not enquire about the tender process. Ask about the organisation's business or strategy, perhaps in the light of any topical developments; or about some aspect of the assignment which has yet to be clarified. That will further underline your interest in the organisation and in the task ahead.

Assessing the presenters

At the rehearsal, the mock panel and observers should make a note of any areas where they believe the team could improve. In particular, the moderator should direct them to the following:

CHECKLIST: Assessing the Presenters

Is the content convincing?

Speakers should be addressing the major issues facing the client, showing how you will help them deal with these issues and how they will benefit through the firm's involvement. Speakers need to include practical examples to illustrate these points.

Do they make a clear case for why your firm should be appointed?

The lead partner should finish with three points that articulate concisely why you are the right firm for the job.

Is the presentation easy to follow?

Each speaker's presentation should be clearly signposted. The points to be covered should be highlighted at the beginning. They should be grouped so that the audience can easily follow the structure, and enumerated as the presentation progresses.

Are the linkages between speakers effective?

You should feel that there is a logical flow between speakers and that they are familiar with each other's material.

Do they come across as a team?

No individual should be too dominant and each participant must have the opportunity to make an impact. The lead partner should explain the role of each member of the team. Each speaker should incorporate cross-references to other team members' input.

Is the presentation concise enough?

As a rule, it is usually best if each individual speaking slot is confined to around five minutes. Unless directed otherwise, the formal presentation should not usually exceed 25 minutes.

Follow-up

Keeping in touch

In many type 2 tenders there is no opportunity to follow-up with the decision-makers after submission of the response or (if applicable) the presentation has been held: you just have to wait for the result. But it is sensible to maintain dialogue with contacts in the organisation where there is scope to do so. You might for example ask them: how they think you fared at the presentation; whether you successfully conveyed the messages you wanted to get across; and if they need the firm to clarify any of the points made.

In some instances you may have your doubts about whether the decision-makers fully understood the points you were making. If during the Q&A you are asked a large number of questions on an issue which you thought was clear-cut, that may indicate that you have not got your message across clearly.

In instances where you are convinced that the organisation did not fully grasp what you were saying (or for whatever reason, you missed out a key part of your proposal), you might consider writing a follow-up letter immediately after the presentation to clarify the area where you may have been misunderstood, or to include the information you left out. Do not do this as a matter of course, however. If it looks as if the decision-makers are happy with what they have been told, making a further unsolicited approach could be counter-productive.

Where it is clear the organisation is having difficulty making a choice, you might suggest to your contacts that that they consider inviting each firm to do something more - such as attend a second presentation or submit further documentation. This will not be necessary in most cases, but it may be helpful where it is apparent that the decision-makers need a tie-break. Taking the initiative in this way may itself give you the edge.

Responding to enquiries

The organisation may need further information from the firm before making its choice. For example, the decision-makers may have been uncertain about your fee structure, or want a more detailed breakdown of your proposed time commitment.

Most requests for additional information are likely to be made via phone or email and in many cases you may be able to provide an answer on the spot, or a few hours later. Of course it will be important to act promptly: the way you tackle these questions will be interpreted as a symbol of how responsive you will be when working on the engagement.

Identifying additional opportunities

Once you have been informed of the decision – and whether you have won or lost – a face-to-face debriefing with the decision-makers to discuss the team's performance in the proposal is likely to be the most effective way to identify other opportunities to work with the organisation. As discussed in chapter 2, it is better if the debrief is conducted by a senior colleague who was not part of the proposal team. At this meeting it may be possible to lay the foundations for future contact – for example, by asking whether the decision-makers want to be on the firm's mailing list or attend its events.

As many tenders occur on two to five-year cycles, contact-building at this stage may put the firm in a stronger position when the work is tendered the next time.

Chapter 7 at a glance:
The Presentation

Context

Face-to-face encounters have the potential to have a greater impact on decision-makers than the written word. But in type 2 tenders the presentation may have a highly restricted role. Bidders need to find out how it fits into the selection process and how much influence it will have in determining the outcome.

Your objectives

The new business pitch is not just an exercise in public speaking. You aim to create a concrete picture of what you will be like to work with, and how you will handle the challenges involved in ensuring your role is a success. As such, it has specific dynamics and objectives that need to be reflected in how you prepare for it.

Reconnaissance

To prepare effectively you need to find out in advance as much as you can about the meeting. For example, it is often helpful to elicit information on: specific topics to focus on in the presentation; who/how many should be included in the presentation team; who will attend from their side; the planned duration of the meeting; and the expected split between the formal part of the presentation and the Q&A.

Selecting the presenters

It is usually safe to assume that the panel will want to see the people who will be most closely involved in delivering the service. Be cautious about taking a figurehead who will not have a role on the assignment, or whose role has not been clearly defined. As a rule, the team should include at least one person below partner level – clients know that associates often do a substantial amount of the work and may be critical to the success of the relationship.

Structure and content

The leader should take responsibility for introducing the team at the start and summing up at the end. Preceding the team introductions with a short scene-setter – perhaps referring to the organisation's objectives and the key challenges of the assignment – can provide a dynamic method of getting the presentation underway.

In the main part of the presentation, the other participants should address the issues raised by the assignment and how the team will achieve the best outcomes for the client. The structure of the points should reflect ISBE principles, as discussed in chapter 5.

The summing up should have a similar role to the summary in the document – highlighting the benefits the client will achieve through the firm's involvement and why the team is well qualified to deliver them.

Delivery

It is better to speak to notes rather than a verbatim script and to use visual aids selectively, if at all. Speech punctuation is a critical aspect of good delivery. This refers to variations in timing, intonation and emphasis that helps to hold the listener's attention and make it easier to assimilate the content.

Signposting is also important. Each speaker should provide a brief overview of the ground he or she intends to cover and enumerate the points as they proceed, to help panel members keep track of the structure.

Team cohesion

One of the most consistent messages to emerge from proposal debriefs is that the ability to come across as a unified team is highly influential in determining the outcome of tenders. A number of methods can be used to strengthen the impression of team cohesion. These include: having the team leader introduce the other members of the presentation team and create a strong platform for the other speakers; ensuring their roles are clearly defined; orchestrating the transitions between speakers; using eye contact; building in cross-references between speakers; and co-ordinating responses to questions.

Preparation and rehearsal

Presentation teams should have a meeting or conference call to discuss the content of the presentation and who is going to cover which topics. The team should physically be together to run through the presentation at two rehearsals. It can be helpful to assemble a mock panel comprising partners not involved in the tender. Participants however need to be carefully briefed and controlled.

The team should pay particular attention to rehearsing the Q&A – regarded by many decision-makers as being more important than the formal part of the presentation.

Follow-up

Keeping in touch with the organisation following the tender can have tactical value. Where appropriate, suggest a follow-up meeting where the discussion with the decision-makers at the presentation appeared to be inconclusive. After the decision has been made, a face-to-face debriefing is likely to be the most effective way to get feedback on the team's performance – and to identify other potential opportunities to work with the organisation.

About the Author

John de Forte has over 30 years' experience of working with legal and other professional services firms on proposals and tenders. This includes advising on and drafting major submissions, helping to develop key messages and maximise the scores from the evaluation. He coaches presentation teams and has developed and conducted a range of training programmes to enable fee-earners to enhance their bidding skills.

His role also includes setting up and reviewing bid departments, carrying out debriefs and gathering intelligence on how bid performance can be improved. In addition to advising firms in the UK, he has worked with bid teams in the US, across Europe and in Asia.

He writes and speaks regularly on tendering and business development. This includes writing a monthly column for Professional Marketing Magazine and contributing to a range of other publications, including the Buying Legal Council's *Legal Procurement Handbook* (available on Amazon). John was one of the first consultants to specialise in advising professional firms on proposals, exploring the challenges which many firms were facing for the first time in his book *Proposals, Pitches and Beauty Parades*, published in 1994 by FT/Pitman.

Outside the legal sector John has worked with a wide range of professionals including global accounting firms and leading providers of actuarial, management consultancy and property management services. He has also helped consortia to win multi-billion pound flagship government contracts in the engineering, construction and other sectors. His role includes acting as editor-in-chief and co-ordinating input from authors in multiple jurisdictions.

www.deforte.com
jdf@deforte.com

About the Buying Legal Council

The international trade organization Buying Legal Council supports professionals tasked with sourcing legal services and managing legal services supplier relationships with advocacy, networking, research, and information.

- We serve as the voice of the profession and promote the interests of buyers of legal services.
- We act as a catalyst in bringing together specialists from all industries and geographies buying legal services.
- We support buyers of legal services through advocacy, networking, research, and information dissemination.
- We advocate for the professionals and promote the value of legal procurement.
- We keep members on top of legal market trends and legal procurement and operations best practices.
- We serve as a bridge between buyers and sellers of legal services.

Our mission is to advance the field of legal procurement, enhance the value and performance of buyers of legal services and their organizations, share intelligence on sourcing legal services and managing supplier relationships, and document and promote best practices.

We identify and provide solutions to both strategic and operational challenges our members face and prepare them for tomorrow's opportunities and challenges. The Buying Legal Council facilitates an innovative dialogue between buyers and sellers of legal services, as well as other stakeholders in the legal market.

Please visit www.buyinglegal.com
Follow us on Twitter: @buyinglegal

Made in the USA
San Bernardino, CA
02 April 2019